ENCOUNTER SERIES

Reinhold Niebuhr Today

Essays by

Richard Wightman Fox
Ralph McInerny
Michael J. Sandel

and
The Story of an Encounter by
Paul T. Stallsworth

Edited and with a Foreword by
Richard John Neuhaus

WILLIAM B. EERDMANS PUBLISHING COMPANY
GRAND RAPIDS, MICHIGAN

Published by Wm. B. Eerdmans Publishing Co.
in cooperation with
The Rockford Institute Center on Religion & Society

Copyright © 1989 by Wm. B. Eerdmans Publishing Co.
255 Jefferson Ave. S.E., Grand Rapids, Mich. 49503

Library of Congress Cataloging-in-Publication Data

Reinhold Niebuhr today / essays by Richard Wightman Fox . . .
   [et al.]; edited and with a Foreword by Richard John Neuhaus.
      p.   cm.   — (The Encounter series; 12)
    ISBN 0-8028-0212-5
    1. Niebuhr, Reinhold, 1892-1971. I. Fox, Richard Wightman,
1945-   . II. Neuhaus, Richard John. III. Series: Encounter series
(Grand Rapids, Mich.); 12.
BX4827.N5N54 1989
230'.092—dc20
                                        89-1486
                                          CIP

For Paul Ramsey

with the gratitude of the participants in this conference,
and of others beyond numbering

Contents

Foreword

Some conferences are very good; a very few are great. This book emerges from what was, in my judgment and the judgment of others, a great conference. It was great in the quality of the presentations, and in the quality of the intense, informed, and civil exchanges among the participants. Of course, the chief ingredient in a good—never mind great—conference is the people who confer. Here the reader will be engaged by the very people whom one would most want to hear on the subject of Reinhold Niebuhr.

In recent years there has been something of a Niebuhr renascence. It has been led in large part by those who are or are suspected of being—as though it were a sin!—neoconservative. Attempting to capture Niebuhr for any partisan agenda, however, would be a great disservice both to Niebuhr and to what he can help us do today. What he can help us do is to reconstitute a religiously grounded public philosophy for the American social and political experiment. Beyond that, he can help us to think clearly about the place of America, and of democracy generally, in our kind of world. Evangelicals, Roman Catholics, fundamentalists, Lutherans, and old-line liberal Protestants very much need Niebuhr today. As you will see, toward the end of the book it is asked whether Niebuhr will be or should be a mentor and model for Christians in the future. The conference participants are not agreed in their answer to that question. But they are agreed—or so it seems to me—that we need to understand the phenomenon that was Reinhold Niebuhr and his astonishing influence on American moral and political discourse.

Richard Fox, whose recent biography of Niebuhr has contributed strongly to the Niebuhr renascence, is sharply challenged for his depiction of Niebuhr's religious beliefs and spirituality. This is an aspect of Niebuhr that is often neglected, so great is the interest in his public role. But it is an aspect closely related to another question that is here explored in depth: What is the theology of the church (ecclesiology) that is needed if Christian moral wisdom is to better serve the *polis*? It will be noted that Stanley Hauerwas is among those who are nervous about putting the question that way. I expect the reader will find that nervousness and the responses to it among the most rewarding parts of this book. (Because of space constraints, it was not possible to include the full text of all the papers prepared for the conference. However, the extended "Story of an Encounter" gives a clear sense of the arguments made and the responses they elicited.)

In the following pages it becomes evident that Paul Ramsey of Princeton was a most spirited participant in this conference. A few months later, in February 1988, Paul Ramsey died at age seventy-four. Confidently commending him to the Lord for whom he lived, we dedicate this book to him. He was a giant among us. When the history of ethics in the twentieth century is written, the person and career of Paul Ramsey will loom large. On general moral theory, on theological ethics, on thought about war and peace, and on moral judgment with respect to medicine and technology, Paul Ramsey led the way that many of us have, however inadequately, tried to follow. A Methodist of generous ecumenical reach, Ramsey showed us the art of argument in service to others whom he respected enough to be impatient with their shoddy thinking. His devotion to Christ and his church was joined to a rigorous scholarship and love for the world that is the object of God's so reckless loving. Ramsey not only understood Niebuhr; he exemplified in our day Niebuhr's knitting together of radical faith and historical responsibility. Even if some of us never took a class with him, Ramsey was the teacher of us all—and not least a teacher of what it means to be a friend. We will not be surprised if, not too long from now, there is another conference and another book titled *Ramsey Today*. In fact, The Center on Religion and Society intends to see to it.

We wish to thank The Pew Charitable Trusts for helping to make this conference possible. And I once again express my gratitude for the indispensable assistance of Paul Stallsworth and Davida Goldman, without whom not much that the Center undertakes would get done.

THE ROCKFORD INSTITUTE   Richard John Neuhaus
CENTER ON RELIGION & SOCIETY
NEW YORK CITY

Niebuhr's World and Ours

Richard Wightman Fox

I

In the epilogue to my biography of Reinhold Niebuhr, I observed that his thought has a distinctively time-bound character. Niebuhr was a deeply incarnational thinker, always testing ideas in action, immersed in the events of his time, launched on a quest for practical wisdom. His brother Richard, his colleague Paul Tillich, and his nemesis Karl Barth all aspired to transcend the particular, the transient, to dwell in the light of the eternal, the ontological, the eschatological. It is easy to imagine them in our midst—still laboring silently at their desks, their faces illumined by the faint glow of sleek word processors as they extend the scaffolding of their systematic frameworks.

It is not so easy to imagine Reinhold in our midst. The social basis for the touring liberal preacher has disappeared. His special forums—the college-chapel circuit, summer assemblies of liberal Christian students, conventions of liberal political and labor cadres — have shrunk in significance. Moreover, he is indelibly associated with certain pivotal events of the middle third of the twentieth century. Our memory of those events is indissolubly linked to our memory of his part in them. Our very habit of employing him as a reference point lengthens the distance that separates him from us. He is a symbol, an emblem, of the liberal struggle in a world

1

of depression, war, and cold war. We remember our past by remembering Niebuhr.[1]

We rightly remember Niebuhr, in the apocryphal phrase long attributed to George Kennan, as "the father of us all." It doesn't really matter whether Kennan said it (he doesn't think he did). For it's true even if he didn't say it. And not just in the sense that Niebuhr was an inspiration for many policy-making political "realists" of the post–World War II period. Niebuhr is also the father of us all in the deeper sense that his confrontation with the events of his time was paradigmatic, a critical model for our generation as a whole. In helping to shape his own world, he helped shape our worldview — above all our inner conviction that all social endeavor is circumscribed by strict limits in a sinful, fragile, imperfect world.[2]

But while acknowledging our inheritance from fathers such as Niebuhr—and there is a strong argument for seeing him as the first among them—we need to honor them by permitting them to pass on. We have to resist the urge to press them into service as if they were our peers. Niebuhr was the product of, and a producer of, a world we have in important respects left behind. His specific social and political stances emerged as parts of an integral response to his world. We cannot tell what he would have thought about abortion, or Star Wars, or the women's movement in the 1980s. To seek his posthumous intervention, to invoke his remembered authority in the debates of our time is usually to dismember him, to cut him out limb by limb from the dense web of his own age.

Of course, much of what Niebuhr said, wrote, and did can be appropriated for our time. He did generalize from his experience, and even when he did not generalize from it, we can do so in retrospect. Even in our post-industrial, post-liberal, postmodern, post-structuralist culture — a culture with little apparent sense of coherence aside from its conviction that it comes *after* something else—certain key insights of this quintessential liberal modernist are directly assimilable. But in this essay I want to stress the point that appropriating Niebuhr demands a

---

1. See my book entitled *Reinhold Niebuhr: A Biography* (New York: Pantheon, 1985), p. 295.

2. On Kennan's famous non-remark, see my *Reinhold Niebuhr*, pp. 238, 319.

careful act of translation, of preservation, of passing beyond dismembering to remembering. We yearn, like the medieval disciples of a departed holy man, to make off with his bones. We need to discipline our impulse to repossess him. We need to appreciate the ways in which he is alien to us, the ways in which his world is not our world. By respecting the pastness of Niebuhr, we can empower ourselves to make the best use of his legacy.

II

How was Niebuhr's world different from our own? One could point to innumerable details of social life and social structure—most obviously to the Great Depression and the burgeoning industrial unionism of the 1930s that Niebuhr promoted and justified for a broad Protestant audience. To remember Niebuhr is to remember the union movement in its heyday. For most of his life the word "justice" —a term constantly on his lips—meant justice for workers, especially industrial workers. Only at the very end of his life did justice come to mean racial justice to the same degree that it meant industrial justice. When Niebuhr tried to give concrete content to his notion of justice, he instinctively thought about equalizing standards of living, reducing job insecurity, and enacting social-insurance schemes. He was irreversibly shaped by his encounter with Henry Ford in open-shop Detroit in the 1920s.

Even in the 1950s, when few former leftists still voiced serious doubts about the justice of the advanced capitalist system, Niebuhr maintained certain reservations. In a 1954 interview, for example, Niebuhr began by making the by-then typical summary of the path he and many of his peers had taken from a "vaguely Marxist orientation" to a "pragmatic" reconciliation with the bourgeois system. His *Children of Light and Children of Darkness* (1944), he said, was his "declaration of independence of all the dogmatic presuppositions on the right and the left. . . . The dogma of the right that justice comes out of freedom was wrong, and . . . the dogma of the left that freedom will come inevitably out of equal justice was equally wrong." He had come to believe that "a pragmatic approach was the only possible democratic approach," that "a free world" had "indeterminate possibilities . . . to solve its problems."

But having reiterated his faith in step-by-step, vital-center democracy, Niebuhr made a point of informing his interviewer that now, in 1954, "capitalism is again too complacent. . . . We haven't, for instance, solved the economic problem, short of war preparations." His pragmatism of mind was still colliding with a visceral, inherited progressivism of spirit: the business community was liable to gain an unfair advantage in the marketplace. This progressive ideology—the view that business was prone to defraud the people, that the people and their neutral, caring, efficient government had to be vigilant to preserve a social equilibrium based on equal opportunity — warred with his conscious wish to move beyond ideology altogether.[3]

In the international sphere the gap between Niebuhr's world and ours is equally apparent. One could point to European events of unparalleled devastation: two world wars, two ignominious defeats for Niebuhr's ancestral homeland, two victories for his country and his wife's (Britain). To remember Niebuhr is to remember his intense engagement in European affairs, his authoritative voice as an interpreter of power politics, his success in persuading a resolutely isolationist Protestant church that military intervention against fascism was the moral necessity of the hour. One suspects that his eminence as a political commentator depended upon an intersection of contingencies: England and Germany, the two foreign nations he knew intimately, both stricken with political and cultural emergencies that he could interpret for and impress upon baffled, inward-looking American audiences. Niebuhr was teacher and preacher. His political analysis, like his religious thinking, was always a campaign of mobilization. His writing, even his most scholarly writing, was the work of a gifted organizer.

Thus, at the simplest level—that of social and political events—Niebuhr's world was centrally marked by gathering labor militancy and by the elemental crises of England and Germany. Those events so dominated Niebuhr's consciousness, so deeply formed his identity, that he seems curiously alien in our day—a time of dwindling faith in the promise of unionization

---

3. From an interview with Niebuhr by Harlan Phillips, May or June 1954, in *The Reminiscences of Reinhold Niebuhr* (New York: Columbia Oral History Research Office, 1972), pp. 65-66.

and of international crisis beyond the frontiers of Western and Central Europe. Of course, it is true that Niebuhr was preoccupied, from World War II on, with both the Soviet Union and Palestine — preoccupations that link him to our era. But in neither case was his very substantial knowledge grounded in personal experience; and in each instance his concern flowed naturally out of his dominant interest in European—especially German and English—affairs. When, especially in later years, he wrote about Asia, he did so with much less insight, and he rarely wrote about Africa and Latin America. His Eurocentrism was typical of his age.

But there is a deeper level—a level beneath the flow of events—at which Niebuhr's world was pronouncedly different from our own. His America was characterized by a much more coherent, well-rooted authority structure than our America. Liberals and conservatives did embrace divergent models of political and economic authority: liberals turned to the paternal state in order to challenge the power of the conservatives' paternal business leadership. But both groups shared a commitment to the paternally governed family as the bedrock of cultural order. "Pragmatic" centrists from liberal and conservative camps could negotiate adjustments in the political and economic realms because they shared a fundamental set of values: the private sphere of home and family and leisure and God was the realm of true human fulfillment; the public (male) sphere of work and politics was the arena of necessity in which compromises, adjustments, and fine-tuning of the machinery of society took place. The widespread consensus on the value-creating character of the private sphere made possible a mirror-image consensus on the utter secularity of the public realm. It was not a place to cultivate ultimate values but a place to effect production, maintain order, and distribute or redistribute opportunity. There were certainly "values" appropriate to the social and political arena, but they were second-order values of tolerance, dispassionate intelligence, and the exercise of judgment in the pursuit of freedom and equality. As Niebuhr always put it, justice, not love, was the goal of the Christian in society.

The liberal Protestant church played a major part in creating and sustaining the authority structure that undergirded Niebuhr's America. The liberal church was a power in its own right—a kind of religious establishment—and also a prime source of ideological support for the parental, caring state, as it had been since the late nineteenth century. After the Civil War, secular (but nevertheless Protestant-informed) liberals such as Henry George began to condemn the effects of free-market liberalism: the immiserization and dependency of "wage slaves" who could no longer aspire to be their own "bosses." Religious liberals such as Washington Gladden and Walter Rauschenbusch also protested against the social forces that destroyed the "personality" of the laboring masses. By the early twentieth century, "liberalism" no longer connoted the laissez-faire faith of Adam Smith but signified the interventionist creed of social reformers who sought to reimpose state controls on the marketplace. Of course, those controls were designed to serve the "public interest," but it is obvious in retrospect that they served not just some abstract public interest, but the particular interest of an emerging professional stratum of technicians and expert helpers.

It is striking to recall that this liberal faith in professional expertise and the caring state—the animating faith of the New Deal synthesis—was largely intact just two decades ago. It was not, as we tend to think, a merely secular vision. Liberal churchmen were vital spokesmen for it. One sign of the power of the vision was precisely its ability to generate religious advocates such as Reinhold Niebuhr and Martin Luther King. Niebuhr's own view (for much of his career) that he was an opponent of "liberalism" must not lead us astray. He did spend decades chipping away at a few well-cemented liberal assumptions about fellowship and love as social strategies or social ends. But he simultaneously (even if for many years unconsciously) was endorsing most cardinal liberal tenets: society as a field of endeavor for human intelligence, the future as a realm of indeterminate possibility, the mind as an adaptive tool for solving practical problems, religion as a social power, culture as a process of inquiry and a cultivation of diversity and toleration, and the state as a forward-looking agent of planning and social equilibrium.[4]

On one level, liberal churchmen like Niebuhr and King

---

4. It is the burden of much of my biography of Niebuhr to reclaim him, against his own self-judgment, for the "liberal" tradition. See, for example, pp. 165-66.

helped legitimize state and professional power by putting it in a theological context; on another level, they pushed that power to go beyond mere efficiency, mere technique, and truly attempt to enact justice and opportunity for the disadvantaged. Underlying Niebuhr's entire adult career was a deep commitment to state-sponsored or state-supported action to reform or transform society. There could be no greater measure of how out of place he would feel in the 1980s, when many liberals have joined conservatives in questioning the capacity of experts, professionals, the state — public authority in general — to discipline and circumscribe private authority.

The authority structure of Niebuhr's era has all but collapsed in our day. The liberal Protestant church has moved, in Jerry Falwell's apt phrase, "from mainline to sideline."[5] Many liberals have apparently abandoned their century-old conviction that the state is the enactor or guarantor of justice and returned in large numbers to the original liberal view that the entrepreneurial ethic not only primes the economic pump but builds moral character. Women have challenged the supremacy of men in both private and public spheres. An enormous watershed located roughly in the decade 1965-1975 separates the authority structure of Niebuhr's age from that of our own. It is no accident that our period lacks a dominant liberal Protestant (male) voice. No one has emerged to take the place of Niebuhr or King—not because liberals lack potential leaders of intelligence and charisma, but because liberal Protestantism, like the broader liberalism of which it forms a part, has fragmented and atrophied.

Liberalism in our day has split into its component parts— the women's movement, the gay rights movement, the antinuclear movement, the sanctuary movement, and others. The civil rights movement of the 1950s and early 1960s, around which all liberals could gather, actually taught separate liberal interest groups how to mobilize themselves and use the media to achieve their particular goals. For most liberals the media have in effect replaced the state as the helping agency of choice. In the aftermath of Vietnam and Watergate, the state lost much of its legitimacy as moral agent. It is the neoconservatives who have taken up the difficult and apparently contradictory task of

---

5. Falwell, quoted by Kenneth L. Woodward in "From 'Mainline' to Sideline," *Newsweek*, 22 Dec. 1986, p. 54.

relegitimizing the state in the post–Vietnam period while still condemning state bureaucracy as inefficient. Liberals have largely abandoned their instinctive reliance on the state; opposition to it is the one thing upon which many of them, divided by their separate interests, can still unite. It puts them in unaccustomed accord with many conservatives—as long as the subject of discussion is limited to domestic affairs. In foreign affairs—debates over liberation theology, for example—nerves are still taut: conservatives leap to their feet and scold antistate liberals for surrendering to the "Vietnam syndrome."

The startling disarray of contemporary liberalism is not just a function of its fragmentation into separate interest groups. It is also the product of an elemental shift in its cultural commitments. If liberals have come to challenge the authority of the state in the public sphere, they have also come increasingly to question the authority of the father-led family in the private sphere. Again, the distance separating Niebuhr from our world is incalculable. There was no more devoted family traditionalist in his era than Niebuhr himself. This was true not only in the sense that Niebuhr's own career came first, and his wife Ursula's came second or not at all. It was also true in the deeper sense that Niebuhr was wedded to a masculine model of authority in the family as the basis of social order in general.

When Niebuhr was a young man, what annoyed him most of all about liberal Protestantism was its effeminate, namby-pamby faith in goodness and love. He felt it wasn't tough enough to contend with evil forces in the "real" world. A study of his rhetorical strategies as a columnist for the *Christian Century* beginning in the 1920s would show how zealously he tried to masculinize Protestant rhetoric — to overwhelm the Victorian niceties of Charles Clayton Morrison with hard-hitting, pointed, hammering prose. A study of his personal friendships with men such as Morrison, John Haynes Holmes, and Waldo Frank would show how difficult it was for him to maintain close personal relationships with his peers: they took too much time, they were passive, they were decorous, they were implicitly feminizing. Niebuhr was a stereotypically masculine leader in a paternalistic era—but an era troubled by the prospect of creeping softness. The liberal movement in effect called him up to a position of authority because he could revitalize it, toughen it, for the social and political struggles of the mid–twentieth century. Today's liberalism has abandoned that commitment to toughness. It would not know what to do with Niebuhr's hard-charging dominance if he were to reappear in our midst. Harvey Cox's recent expression of sadness at Niebuhr's failure to learn the art of friendship is a revealing sign of the distance between our generation of liberals and Niebuhr's.[6]

Frances FitzGerald's recent *Cities on a Hill* is a brilliant analysis of the liberal turnabout on the family and paternal authority. Of the four "contemporary cultures" she studies, only one — Jerry Falwell's Lynchburg church and "university" — preserves a firm commitment to the traditional nuclear, paternally managed family. The other three—the Castro gay community in San Francisco, the Sun City retirement community in Florida, and the now-defunct Rajneeshpuram commune in Oregon—are vanguard examples, in her view, of the reorientation of liberal culture. All three are grounded upon the pursuit of therapeutic "growth" for adults who have selected their lifestyle of choice, a lifestyle that protects them from any responsibility to oversee the growth of children—that is, the cultivation of the next generation.

These lifestyle "enclaves," to use Robert Bellah's term, in the realm of leisure are the mirror images of the separate liberal political-interest groups in the realm of power-seeking. Lifestyle enclaves may themselves be highly politicized—as in the case of the Castro gay community—but it is the politics of the single interest group. What unites the liberal enclaves — whether politicized or not—is their rejection of the paternalistic family, just as what unites many of the liberal interest groups is their rejection of the paternalistic state. But this abstract ideological unity goes hand in hand with a striking institutional and programmatic diversity. Liberalism is decentralized both in the pursuit of power and in the pursuit of the good life.[7]

Nothing would have been more upsetting to Niebuhr, had he lived into our era, than the further development of the ideol-

6. Cox, "Theology, Politics, and Friendship," *Christianity and Crisis*, 3 Feb. 1986, pp. 16-18.

7. FitzGerald, *Cities on a Hill: A Journey through Four Contemporary American Cultures* (New York: Simon & Schuster, 1986); Bellah et al., *Habits of the Heart: Individualism and Commitment in American Life* (Berkeley: University of California Press, 1984).

ogy of personal "growth." He knew, in the 1950s, that this
therapeutic consumerism was spreading: he had only to con-
template the rise of his colleague Paul Tillich to the ironic position of celebrity moralist—ironic not only because Tillich was a
systematic theologian, not an ethicist, but also because he was
promiscuous to the point of neurosis in his dealings with
women. Niebuhr had learned to wince when he heard Tillich
utter the word "responsibility": to Niebuhr it connoted self-
sacrificial, long-term labor for justice in the social sphere; to Tillich it connoted self-development, including the development
of one's senses, one's body, and one's pleasures. But by now
even Tillich is passé: he is too cerebral for a generation that im-
agines it no longer has to work itself out of feelings of guilt and
anxiety—a generation that has no idea that it requires, as Tillich
put it, "courage to be."

III

Most liberals in Niebuhr's day shared a firm faith in the
authority of the state and the authority of the family. Most
liberals in our "post-liberal" era have faith in neither. But there
is a third way in which Niebuhr's world is not our world.
Liberals in his time could still agree upon the proposition that
mind, intelligence, could unravel the mysteries of nature and
pierce the veils of social obfuscation. Reason could reach out to
things in themselves, then deliberate on the proper means of ordering, mastering, and reforming them. The imperial intellect
confronted serious obstacles, including its own biases and often
outdated assumptions, but when subjected to critical discipline,
it could in principle attain and contain its objective: the hard
facts of reality.

Niebuhr was more sensitive than most liberals to the
biases that subverted reason. Indeed, he often sounded like an
irrationalist who doubted that reason could ever rise above self-
ish interest to the heights of true understanding. But his attacks
on reason, like his attacks on liberal sentimentality and
utopianism, were intraliberal polemics designed to sharpen
liberal awareness of the dangers of complacency. He was as
devoted to rational analysis as John Dewey, even when he
mocked Dewey's alleged belief in the sufficiency of reason alone
to remake the world. In Niebuhr's mind the problem with lib-

erals was not their devotion to reason but their eagerness to check their reason at the door when they entered the make-believe palaces of their fond ideals. He wanted more reason, sharper reason, more uncompromising reason to penetrate the mystifications of all ideologies, whether of the right or the left. Liberal ideals were prone to cover up, not illuminate, reality. The task of the prophet was to tear off the drapery and expose the real to searing, blinding light.

The post-liberal period has by no means wholly abandoned the liberal view of inner mind and outer world. Liberals like Noam Chomsky and Michael Harrington still aspire to unveil, expose, and refashion the pre-existing, objective realities of the social arena. But a sizable contingent of liberal intellectual leaders — most notably, perhaps, the anthropologist Clifford Geertz and the philosopher Richard Rorty (who with perfect irony happens to be the grandson of liberal Social Gospeller Walter Rauschenbusch)—have to varying degrees given up on the realist epistemology of the older liberalism.

For Geertz the subject of anthropology becomes not the "primitive" culture itself but the encounter between the anthropologist and that culture. Cultures are not objects to be scrutinized and measured, but webs, grids, and texts that must be "read" by a reader whose knowledge of the language is imperfect. The key problem of anthropology becomes the problem of interpretation; hermeneutics takes priority over collecting and ordering data from the external world. Likewise, for Rorty the subject of philosophy becomes not the external world itself but the conversations that people have about their ideas, traditions, and languages. His new "pragmatism" finds truth not in the investigation of nature but in the conventions and discourses that human communities construct for their edification. Philosophy is about talking together, not about some pre-existing "reality." The true is what "works" in solving problems — including the intellectual problems of the academic disciplines. The pursuit of truth is the manipulation of texts and contexts; it has no outside referent in the natural world.

Geertz and Rorty do not go as far as some literary postmodernists and post-structuralists in reducing reality to textuality. They are sensitive to the *social* construction of reality; reality is historical, a product of human interaction. But they nevertheless represent a key shift in the liberal sensibility. For them intellectual work is a much more skeptical, self-critical, hermeneutical enterprise than it was for their liberal predecessors. It is no longer an effort to measure and master the external realm of facticity.[8]

"Post-liberal" theologians seem to share a good deal with their post-modern peers in the other human sciences. Of course, unlike Rorty and Geertz, the theologians claim to be in touch with ultimate reality. Or rather, they still believe that the problem of how we might conceive ourselves to be in touch with such a reality remains a vital question. Where they differ from the liberal theologians of Niebuhr's era, and implicitly agree with other post-modernists, is in their insistence on textuality, on the language of faith. Theologians such as George Lindbeck and Stanley Hauerwas reject the starting point of liberal apologetics: that Christian stories can and should be translated into modern terms so that modern scientific men and women can make sense of them and be led by them to the ultimate encounter.[9]

The post-liberal theologians would appear to be building on the perspective of H. Richard Niebuhr, whose *Meaning of Revelation* (1941) was itself a rejection of much of liberal modernism—including much of the liberal modernism of his brother Reinhold. He despised the liberal tendency—a tendency that strongly marked his brother's work—to reduce Christianity to a philosophy of life, to a search for "meaningfulness" in human existence. For him God was truly an actor in history, truly "real," not simply an idea which modern Christians found it useful to embrace because it made more sense out of life than alternative beliefs. But God was encountered only in the light of faith, not

---

8. Geertz, *The Interpretation of Cultures* (New York: Basic Books, 1973); Rorty, *Philosophy and the Mirror of Nature* (Princeton: Princeton University Press, 1979), and *Consequences of Pragmatism: Essays, 1972-1980* (Minneapolis: University of Minnesota Press, 1982). On the Geertzian turn in anthropology, see George E. Marcus and Michael M. J. Fischer, *Anthropology as Cultural Critique: An Experimental Moment in the Human Sciences* (Chicago: University of Chicago Press, 1986). On the Rortian turn in philosophy—a turn much appreciated in post-structuralist circles — see Frank Lentricchia, *Criticism and Social Change* (Chicago: University of Chicago Press, 1983), pp. 1-20.

9. Lindbeck, *The Nature of Doctrine* (Philadelphia: Westminster Press, 1984); Hauerwas, *Peaceable Kingdom: A Primer in Christian Ethics* (Notre Dame, Ind.: University of Notre Dame Press, 1983).

reason. Richard Niebuhr anticipated the post-liberal world in his skepticism about the power of reason to illuminate the ultimately real.

His task was to reflect upon the Christian tradition itself, to take it as given, to develop its internal resources and pass it on, enriched and integral, to later generations. In that respect he is the direct precursor of the contemporary post-liberals. Like them, he avoided skepticism, paradoxically, by embracing a certain relativism. The Christian tradition offers *one* well-developed path for reaching into the unknown and awaiting the hand of God. It is a unique faith but not the only true faith. The Christian's main job is not to convert the heathen. That traditional endeavor, characteristic of both liberals and conservative fundamentalists, leads to an inevitable dilution of the faith to make it palatable. For the post-liberals, the Christian's task is to preserve an inheritance.

From Reinhold's standpoint, his brother's perspective was too resigned, too passive, too ready to abandon the world to its sins. He would probably have had equal difficulty accepting the theology of the post-liberals. Their stance would have struck him as insufficiently secular, too churchy, too timid about using the world's methods to reshape the world. He would have bemoaned its refusal to absorb and rekindle the secular liberal agenda. For him post-liberal theology would have amounted to a withdrawal from public concerns, a privatization of faith. It might well have struck him as a sign that the church was losing its muscularity, its cultural power, and becoming one more in a series of lifestyle enclaves.

IV

If Reinhold Niebuhr is in important respects alien to us, if his world is not our world, if his life and thought were rooted in a context we have in many ways left behind—we can nevertheless appropriate him for our time. Above all he is significant to us as both exponent and critic of public theology, which is today in full renewal not only in the theological arena but in the work of certain ostensibly secular neoliberals such as Robert Bellah and the other authors of *Habits of the Heart*.

The "Bellah bunch," as historian Robert Westbrook has dubbed them, are a significant cultural phenomenon in their own right. They are a telling sign of the desire shared by many liberals to reconceive and reintegrate the liberal vision. They are also a contemporary phenomenon that Reinhold Niebuhr would have recognized in an instant: they are the resurrection, despite their professional and social scientific credentials, of liberal Protestant social theory. No doubt if he were here, he would launch a sharp critique of their faith in the basic goodness of human beings, in the fundamental fit between intelligent individuals and the society they are capable of building. But their work also amounts to a strong challenge to Niebuhr's public theology. A "dialogue" (Bellah's key term) between their perspective and Niebuhr's would sharpen both, and take contemporary liberals a long way toward restoring their vision— and perhaps even their politics.

Niebuhr's public theology was a paradoxical mix of secular and religious conviction. On one level it was firmly, zealously secular. By the late 1920s he had developed an intense aversion to the notion of a "Christian" politics—or a politics imbued with any other "religious" faith, including communism. The liberal Protestant quest for an integral moral community, for a society conceived as a fellowship, was a delusion. In *Moral Man and Immoral Society* (1932) he heaped scorn on that vision. Industrial society was not a field for cultivating moral harmony but a pluralistic realm of power blocs and interest groups. The ethical task was to adjudicate interests, redistribute social benefits, attain a new (though always temporary) equilibrium of justice.

But Niebuhr's public theology was also deeply religious —in two senses. First, his vision of the secular world as a field of colliding, self-interested units flowed out of his biblical understanding of human nature. The sinful self, whatever its pretensions to goodness and sociability, was always prone to put itself first. The will to power pushed through even the most humble convictions. Second, his vision was religious in that he believed that the secular world could not simply be left to itself: it had to be judged, challenged by the biblical commitment to justice. A pluralist democracy depended for moral sustenance upon belief in the transcendent God, from whose standpoint all human beings were both valuable and responsible. The secular world, therefore, had to be protected against invasion by self-righteous "religious" parties, but it also had to be provoked, unsettled by a religious perspective. Pure secularity was degenerative: it moved inexorably toward the jungle warfare of all against all, followed in all likelihood by an imposed social stabilization sponsored by reactionary forces of order.

There is a fundamental ambiguity in Niebuhr's public theology. On the one hand, he is persuaded that America is morally pluralistic, united only by a shared belief in the (secular) "open society." On the other hand, he suggests that the open society will flourish only if it is grounded in a prior (religious) consensus, a belief in the transcendent God. Niebuhr wriggles out of the inconsistency by avoiding the question of how a religious consensus could be constructed in a culturally heterogeneous society. He affirms instead his own and other Christians' prophetic responsibility to judge secular society, to force it to embody a tension between social peace and social justice. Niebuhr's own identity as Christian man-of-the-world, as religious-secular leader par excellence, was a brilliant enactment, at the personal level, of his own public theology. The secular world was a realm of value, but its reserves of virtue were limited and had to be replenished by religion — not the religion of the churches, which Niebuhr always regarded as tepid and complacent, but the religion of the prophets.

The authors of *Habits of the Heart* contend that the secular world possesses two different reservoirs of value: the biblical tradition and the republican tradition. From their standpoint, Niebuhr is right about the significance of biblical, prophetic critique, but wrong to minimize the potential for virtue that lies within secular society itself. According to the republican tradition, freedom resides not in the pursuit of self-interest — the liberal, marketplace goal to which Niebuhr tends to reduce the whole notion of secularity—but in the collective, participatory deliberations of the *polis*. Liberty is not isolated, individual activity but the autonomous activity that grows out of common engagement in chosen tasks. Real freedom means self-expression *and* self-limitation. There is no individual fulfillment that is not informed by the discipline of some group, which alone knows how to recognize and revere individual excellence. There is no individual growth that is not also the growth of a community or set of communities.

The great strength of *Habits of the Heart* is its perception that self-realization and communal realization are intertwined. Bellah's vision is fundamentally Rousseauian and Durkheimian:

the negative freedom of the classical liberal tradition—freedom from the state, the polity, the group—is replaced by the positive freedom of the republican tradition. But Bellah is also a contemporary liberal who cannot follow Rousseau in viewing the state as the ultimate custodian of communal virtue, or follow Durkheim in positing a state-regulated system of occupational guilds within which merely individual impulses can be disciplined and molded. He therefore has embraced Alasdair MacIntyre's *After Virtue* as a means of reconceiving the "public" as a set of individual and group "practices" that are independent of the state.[10]

For Niebuhr, as for the other liberals of his generation, the state was the ultimate broker, the disciplinary agency of choice. It was in fact his belief in the state as actual or potential moral guarantor that permitted Niebuhr to place his faith in prophecy instead of putting it in the slow building of moral consensus: the prophet could mobilize opinion and spark state intervention on behalf of justice. Bellah no longer has that option. He must hold out for the creation of a new consensus; that is the only way, in the absence of a legitimate state, to relegitimize the "public," the communal. But, like Niebuhr, he is a pluralist who winces at the prospect of moral uniformity. He therefore looks for a kind of consensus that does not imply homogeneity but that does imply solidarity and fellowship. He enacts a procedural, formal consensus based on "dialogue," "conversation," "participation." The solidarity he apparently has in mind will ultimately become more than a formal category: as participants develop the "callings," realize themselves in expanding webs of long-term social relationships, they will create a new culture that combines diversity of belief with consensus of commitment. Their intense commitment to the process of self-realization and communal realization will itself amount to a substantive, organic sharing.

Bellah's perspective offers an important corrective to Niebuhr's. The key threat to freedom in modern society is not some imbalance of political forces but an atrophy of community life. The problem is cultural before it is political—or rather, the political problem is at bottom a cultural one. The pursuit of justice can no longer be undertaken without a simultaneous pur-

---

10. MacIntyre, *After Virtue* (Notre Dame, Ind.: University of Notre Dame Press, 1981).

suit of collective self-expression. The pursuers of justice must first pursue a culture of democratic deliberation. The process by which justice is sought is critical; equality can be attained only if it is acted out all along the way.

Bellah's stance also offers a corrective to the post-modern liberalism of Richard Rorty, whose cultural "conversation" stops short of pursuing any kind of social transformation. Rorty's dialogue—despite its abandonment of the notion of a pre-existing external reality—is in principle capable of accommodating social action in pursuit of justice: like the turn-of-the-century pragmatists, Rorty dispenses with ontology and metaphysics, but not with the social creation of a reality-for-us. But Rorty chooses to accentuate the apolitical applications of his perspective: the point is to master the conventions of one's discourse, to learn to work and play with pleasure and humility within those historically generated bounds. The point of philosophy is to understand one's tradition, not to change or understand the external world.[11]

To Niebuhr, Bellah's position would look like warmed-over liberal Protestant utopianism: love, fellowship, and goodwill as the keys to kingdom-building. There is a Pollyannaish tone to Bellah's work, but Niebuhr's reading of it would be a misconstrual. Niebuhr was not sufficiently sensitive to the pivotal place that a theory of self-realization must occupy in a democratic culture. He was too prone to reduce the democratic problem to the task of redistributing power.

Yet Niebuhr's realism nevertheless suggests an important corrective to Bellah's neoliberal quest. Bellah's participatory citizens are too uniformly good-natured. They are liberal versions of the proletarian he-men of the socialist realism of the 1930s: earnest, sincere, articulate, deliberative, willing to compromise, tolerant of other views, determined to see the good and do it. There is no elemental conflict in Bellah's model of the good soul or the good society—no Pauline sense that a law in one's members wars against the law in one's mind, that the good I would do, I do not. There is just the occasional disagreement among friends.

From Niebuhr's standpoint, individuals are always liable

---

11. On the political standpattism of Rorty's liberalism, see William E. Connolly, "Mirror of America," *Raritan* 3 (Summer 1983): 124-35.

to undermine collective enterprises out of pride and selfishness. Likewise, one group attempts to subordinate or discredit another group. All human endeavors—even the most holy, righteous, or cooperative—are riddled with calculations of interest and deceit. Bellah, like the whole republican tradition he is drawing on, tends to assume that individuals gather harmoniously in society—at least in principle. They may lose their virtue over time through the depredations of jealousy and self-aggrandizement, but that loss is not inevitable. Individuals are not in any essential sense at odds with society. Niebuhr, like Freud, knows better. The great contribution Niebuhr still has to make to liberal theory is to insist *both* that the built-in human will-to-power is a perennial reality of social life, a permanent obstacle to lofty communal dreams, *and* that prophets great and small must still labor for structural social transformations. Social progress is possible, even if it is fragile, hesitant, nonlinear.

Niebuhr's perspective would be even more useful if he had worked out a theory of public virtue—a theory that is implicit in some of his work, especially in the second volume of *The Nature and Destiny of Man* (1943). Likewise, Bellah's position would be more useful if he appropriated some of Niebuhr's realism about human nature. Building a new liberal consensus will require not just a new theory but a long-term cultural transformation. And Niebuhr's realism can supply a good dose of stoic resolve—and stoic humor—for the absurdities and challenges that are sure to be encountered in the decades to come.

The Political Theory of the Procedural Republic*

Michael J. Sandel

My aim is to connect a certain debate in political theory with a certain development in our political practice. The debate is the one between rights-based liberalism and its communitarian, or civic republican, critics. The development is the advent in the United States of what might be called the "procedural republic," a public life animated by the rights-based liberal ethic. In the modern American welfare state, it seems, the liberal dimensions of our tradition have crowded out the republican dimensions, with adverse consequences for the democratic prospect and the legitimacy of the regime.

In this essay I will first identify the liberal and civic republican theories at issue in contemporary political philosophy, and then employ these contrasting theories in an interpretation of the American political condition. I hope ultimately to show that we can illuminate our political practice by identifying the contending political theories and self-images it embodies. This essay is a preliminary effort in that direction.

I

Liberals often take pride in defending what they oppose—por-

---

*This paper also appears in *The Rule of Law,* which is edited by Allan C. Hutchinson and Patrick J. Monahan (Toronto: Carswell, 1987).

nography, for example, or unpopular views.[1] They say the state should not impose on its citizens a preferred way of life, but should leave them as free as possible to choose their own values and ends, consistent with a similar liberty for others. This commitment to freedom of choice requires that liberals constantly distinguish between permission and praise, between allowing a practice and endorsing it. It is one thing to allow pornography, they argue, and something else to affirm it.

Conservatives sometimes exploit this distinction by ignoring it. They charge that those who would allow abortions favor abortion, that opponents of school prayer oppose prayer, that those who defend the rights of communists sympathize with their cause. And in a pattern of argument familiar in our politics, liberals reply by invoking higher principles: it is not that they dislike pornography less, but rather that they more highly value toleration, or freedom of choice, or fair procedures.

But in contemporary debate, the liberal rejoinder seems increasingly fragile, its moral basis increasingly unclear. Why should toleration and freedom of choice prevail when other important values are also at stake? Too often the answer implies some version of moral relativism, the idea that it is wrong to "legislate morality" because all morality is merely subjective. "Who is to say what is literature and what is filth? That is a value judgment, and whose values should decide?"

Relativism usually appears less as a claim than as a question. ("Who is to judge?") But it is a question that can also be asked of the values that liberals defend. Toleration and freedom and fairness are values too, and they can hardly be defended by the claim that no values can be defended. So it is a mistake to affirm liberal values by arguing that all values are merely subjective. The relativist defense of liberalism is no defense at all.

What, then, can be the moral basis of the higher principles the liberal invokes? Recent political philosophy has offered two main alternatives — one utilitarian, the other Kantian. The utilitarian view, following John Stuart Mill, defends liberal principles in the name of maximizing the general welfare. The state should not impose on its citizens a preferred way of life, even

---

1. In this and the following section, I draw on my introduction to the book I edited entitled *Liberalism and Its Critics* (Oxford: Basil Blackwell, 1984).

for their own good, because doing so will reduce the sum of human happiness, at least in the long run; better that people choose for themselves, even if, on occasion, they get it wrong. "The only freedom which deserves the name," writes Mill, "is that of pursuing our own good in our own way, so long as we do not attempt to deprive others of theirs, or impede their efforts to obtain it." He adds that his argument does not depend on any notion of abstract right, only on the principle of the greatest good for the greatest number. "I regard utility as the ultimate appeal on all ethical questions; but it must be utility in the largest sense, grounded on the permanent interests of man as a progressive being."[2]

Many objections have been raised against utilitarianism as a general doctrine of moral philosophy. Some have questioned the concept of utility, and the assumption that all human goods are in principle commensurable. Others have objected that by reducing all values to preferences and desires, utilitarians are unable to admit qualitative distinctions of worth, unable to distinguish noble desires from base ones. But most recent debate has focused on whether utilitarianism offers a convincing basis for liberal principles, including respect for individual rights.

In one respect, utilitarianism would seem well-suited to liberal purposes. Maximizing utility does not require judging people's values, only aggregating them. And the willingness to aggregate preferences without judging them suggests a tolerant spirit, even a democratic one. When people go to the polls, we count their votes, whatever they are.

But the utilitarian calculus is not always as liberal as it first appears. If enough cheering Romans pack the Coliseum to watch the lion devour the Christian, the collective pleasure of the Romans will surely outweigh the pain of the Christian, intense though it be. Or if a big majority abhors a small religion and wants it banned, the balance of preferences will favor suppression, not toleration. Utilitarians sometimes defend individual rights on the grounds that respecting them now will serve utility in the long run. But this calculation is precarious and contingent. It hardly secures the liberal promise not to impose on some the values of others. Just as the majority will is an

---

2. Mill, *On Liberty,* ed. Elizabeth Rapaport (Indianapolis: Hackett Publishing Co., 1978), chap. 1.

inadequate instrument of liberal politics — by itself it fails to secure individual rights—so the utilitarian philosophy is an inadequate foundation for liberal principles.

The case against utilitarianism was made most powerfully by Kant. He argued that empirical principles such as utility were unfit to serve as the basis for the moral law. A wholly instrumental defense of freedom and rights not only leaves rights vulnerable but fails to respect the inherent dignity of persons. The utilitarian calculus treats people as means to the happiness of others, not as ends in themselves, worthy of respect.[3]

Contemporary liberals extend Kant's argument with the claim that utilitarianism fails to take seriously the distinction between persons. In seeking above all to maximize the general welfare, utilitarianism treats society as a whole as if it were a single person; it conflates our many, diverse desires into a single system of desires. It is indifferent to the distribution of satisfactions among persons, except insofar as this may affect the overall sum. But this fails to respect our plurality and distinctness. It uses some as means to the happiness of all, and so fails to respect each as an end in himself.

Modern-day Kantians reject the utilitarian approach in favor of an ethic that takes rights more seriously. In their view, certain rights are so fundamental that even the general welfare cannot override them. As John Rawls writes, "Each person possesses an inviolability founded on justice that even the welfare of society as a whole cannot override. . . . The rights secured by justice are not subject to political bargaining or to the calculus of social interests."[4]

So Kantian liberals need an account of rights that does not depend on utilitarian considerations. More than this, they need an account that does not depend on any particular conception of the good, that does not presuppose the superiority of one way of life over others. Only a justification neutral about ends could

---

3. See Kant, *Groundwork of the Metaphysics of Morals,* trans. H. J. Paton (New York: Harper & Row, 1956), and "On the Common Saying: 'This May Be True in Theory, But It Does Not Apply in Practice,' " in *Kant's Political Writings,* ed. Hans Reiss (Cambridge: Cambridge University Press, 1970).

4. Rawls, *A Theory of Justice* (Oxford: Oxford University Press, 1971), pp. 3-4.

preserve the liberal resolve not to favor any particular ends, or to allow the state to impose on its citizens a preferred way of life. But what sort of justification could this be? How is it possible to affirm certain liberties and rights as fundamental without embracing some vision of the good life, without endorsing some ends over others? It would seem we are back to the relativist predicament — to affirm liberal principles without embracing any particular ends.

The solution proposed by Kantian liberals is to draw a distinction between the "right" and the "good"—between a framework of basic rights and liberties, and the conceptions of the good that people may choose to pursue within that framework. It is one thing for the state to support a fair framework, Kantian liberals argue, and something else to affirm some particular ends. For example, it is one thing to defend the right to free speech so that people may be free to form their own opinions and choose their own ends, but something else to support this right on the grounds that a life of political discussion is inherently worthier than a life unconcerned with public affairs, or on the grounds that free speech will increase the general welfare. Only the first defense is available in the Kantian view, resting as it does on the ideal of a neutral framework.

Now the commitment to a framework neutral among ends can be seen as a kind of value—in this sense the Kantian liberal is no relativist—but its value consists precisely in its refusal to affirm a preferred way of life or conception of the good. For Kantian liberals, then, the right is prior to the good, and in two senses. First, individual rights cannot be sacrificed for the sake of the general good, and second, the principles of justice that specify these rights cannot be premised on any particular vision of the good life. What justifies the rights is not that they maximize the general welfare or otherwise promote the good, but rather that they comprise a fair framework within which individuals and groups can choose their own values and ends, consistent with a similar liberty for others.

Of course, proponents of the rights-based ethic notoriously disagree about what rights are fundamental, and about what political arrangements the ideal of the neutral framework requires. Egalitarian liberals support the welfare state and favor a scheme of civil liberties together with certain social and economic rights—rights to welfare, education, health care, and so on. Libertarian liberals defend the market economy and claim that redistributive policies violate people's rights; they favor a scheme of civil liberties combined with a strict regime of private property rights. But whether egalitarian or libertarian, rights-based liberalism begins with the claim that we are separate, individual persons, each with our own aims, interests, and conceptions of the good, and it seeks a framework of rights that will enable us to realize our capacity as free moral agents, consistent with a similar liberty for others.

II

Within academic philosophy, the last decade or so has seen the ascendance of the rights-based ethic over the utilitarian one, due in large part to the influence of John Rawls' important work, *A Theory of Justice*. In the debate between utilitarian and rights-based theories, the rights-based ethic has come to prevail. The legal philosopher H. L. A. Hart recently described the shift from "the old faith that some form of utilitarianism must capture the essence of political morality" to the new faith that "the truth must lie with a doctrine of basic human rights, protecting specific basic liberties and interests of individuals. . . . Whereas not so long ago great energy and much ingenuity of many philosophers were devoted to making some form of utilitarianism work, latterly such energies and ingenuity have been devoted to the articulation of theories of basic rights."[5]

But in philosophy as in life, the new faith becomes the old orthodoxy before long. Even as it has come to prevail over its utilitarian rival, the rights-based ethic has recently faced a growing challenge from a different direction, from a view that gives fuller expression to the claims of citizenship and community than the liberal vision allows. Recalling the arguments of Hegel against Kant, the communitarian critics of modern liberalism question the claim for the priority of the right over the good and the picture of the freely choosing individual it embodies. Following Aristotle, they argue that we cannot justify political arrangements without reference to common purposes and ends,

---

5. Hart, "Between Utility and Rights," in *The Idea of Freedom*, ed. Alan Ryan (Oxford: Oxford University Press, 1979), p. 77.

and that we cannot conceive our personhood without reference to our role as citizens and as participants in a common life. This debate reflects two contrasting pictures of the self. The rights-based ethic and the conception of the person it embodies were shaped in large part in the encounter with utilitarianism. Where utilitarians conflate our many desires into a single system of desire, Kantians insist on the separateness of persons. Where the utilitarian self is simply defined as the sum of its desires, the Kantian self is a choosing self, independent of the desires and ends it may have at any moment. As Rawls writes, "The self is prior to the ends which are affirmed by it; even a dominant end must be chosen from among numerous possibilities."[6]

The priority of the self over its ends means I am never defined by my aims and attachments but am always capable of standing back to survey and assess and possibly to revise them. This is what it means to be a free and independent self, capable of choice. And this is the vision of the self that finds expression in the ideal of the state as a neutral framework. On the rights-based ethic, it is precisely because we are essentially separate, independent selves that we need a neutral framework, a framework of rights that refuses to choose among competing purposes and ends. If the self is prior to its ends, then the right must be prior to the good.

Communitarian critics of rights-based liberalism say we cannot conceive ourselves as independent in this way, as bearers of selves wholly detached from our aims and attachments. They say that certain of our roles are partly constitutive of the persons we are—as citizens of a country, or members of a movement, or partisans of a cause. But if we are partly defined by the communities we inhabit, then we must also be implicated in the purposes and ends characteristic of those communities. As Alasdair MacIntyre writes, "What is good for me has to be the good for one who inhabits these roles."[7] Open-ended though it be, the story of my life is always embedded in the story of those communities from which I derive my identity—whether family or city, people or nation, party or cause. In the communitarian

---

6. Rawls, *A Theory of Justice*, p. 560.
7. MacIntyre, *After Virtue* (Notre Dame: University of Notre Dame Press, 1981), p. 205.

view, these stories make a moral difference, not only a psychological one. They situate us in the world and give our lives their moral particularity.

What is at stake for politics in the debate between unencumbered selves and situated ones? What are the practical differences between a politics of rights and a politics of the common good? On some issues the two theories may produce different arguments for similar policies. For example, the civil rights movement of the 1960s might be justified by liberals in the name of human dignity and respect for persons, and by communitarians in the name of recognizing the full membership of fellow citizens wrongly excluded from the common life of the nation. And where liberals might support public education in hopes of equipping students to become autonomous individuals, capable of choosing their own ends and pursuing them effectively, communitarians might support public education in hopes of equipping students to become good citizens, capable of contributing meaningfully to public deliberations and pursuits.

On other issues the two ethics might lead to different policies. Communitarians would be more likely than liberals to allow a town to ban pornographic bookstores, on the grounds that pornography offends the town's way of life and the values that sustain it. But a politics of civic virtue does not always part company with liberalism in favor of conservative policies. For example, communitarians would be more willing than some rights-oriented liberals to see states enact laws regulating plant closings in order to protect their communities from the disruptive effects of capital mobility and sudden industrial change. More generally, where the liberal regards the expansion of individual rights and entitlements as unqualified moral and political progress, the communitarian is troubled by the tendency of liberal programs to displace politics from smaller forms of association to more comprehensive ones. Where libertarian liberals defend the private economy and egalitarian liberals defend the welfare state, communitarians worry about the concentration of power in both the corporate economy and the bureaucratic state, and the erosion of those intermediate forms of community that have at times sustained a more vital public life.

Liberals often argue that a politics of the common good, drawing as it must on particular loyalties, obligations, and traditions, opens the way to prejudice and intolerance. The modern nation-state is not the Athenian *polis*, they point out; the scale and diversity of modern life have rendered the Aristotelian political ethic nostalgic at best and dangerous at worst. Any attempt to govern by a vision of the good is likely to lead to a slippery slope of totalitarian temptations.

Communitarians reply that intolerance flourishes most where forms of life are dislocated, roots unsettled, traditions undone. In our day the totalitarian impulse has sprung less from the convictions of confidently situated selves than from the confusions of atomized, dislocated, frustrated selves, at sea in a world where common meanings have lost their force. As Hannah Arendt has written, "What makes mass society so difficult to bear is not the number of people involved, or at least not primarily, but the fact that the world between them has lost its power to gather them together, to relate and to separate them."[8] Insofar as our public life has withered, our sense of common involvement diminished, we lie vulnerable to the mass politics of totalitarian solutions. So responds the party of the common good to the party of rights. If the party of the common good is right, our most pressing moral and political project is to revitalize those civic republican possibilities implicit in our tradition but fading in our time.

III

How might the contrast between the liberal and communitarian, or civic republican, theories we have been considering help illuminate our present political condition? We might begin by locating these theories in the political history of the American republic. Both the liberal and the republican conceptions have been present throughout, but in differing measures and with shifting importance. Broadly speaking, the republican strand was most evident from the time of the founding of this country to the late nineteenth century; by the mid- to late twentieth century, the liberal conception came increasingly to predominate, gradually crowding out republican dimensions. In this section I shall try to identify three moments in the transition from the re-

---

8. Arendt, *The Human Condition: A Study of the Central Dilemmas Facing Modern Man* (Chicago: University of Chicago Press, 1958), pp. 52-53.

publican to the liberal constitutional order: (1) the civic republic, (2) the national republic, and (3) the procedural republic.

A. The Civic Republic

The ideological origins of American politics is the subject of lively and voluminous debate among intellectual historians. Some emphasize the Lockean liberal sources of American political thought, others the civic republican influences.[9] But beyond the question of who influenced the founders' thought is the further question of what kind of political life they actually lived. It is clear that the assumptions embodied in the practice of eighteenth-century American politics, the ideas and institutions that together constitute the "civic republic," differ from those of the modern liberal political order in several respects.

First, liberty in the civic republic was defined not in opposition to democracy, as an individual's guarantee against what the majority might will, but as a function of democracy, of democratic institutions and dispersed power. In the eighteenth century, civil liberty referred not to a set of personal rights in the sense of immunities, as in the modern "right to privacy," but, in Hamilton's words, "to a share in the government." Civil liberty was public, or political, liberty, "equivalent to democracy or government by the people themselves." It was not primarily individual, but "the freedom of bodies politic, or States."[10]

Second, the terms of relation between the individual and the nation were not direct and unmediated; they were indirect and mediated by decentralized forms of political association, participation, and allegiance. As Laurence Tribe points out, "It was

---

9. For examples of the liberal view, see Louis Hartz, *The Liberal Tradition in America* (New York: Harcourt Brace, 1955), and, more recently, Isaac Kramnick, "Republican Revisionism Revisited," *American Historical Review* 87 (1982), and John Diggins, *The Lost Soul of American Politics: Virtue, Self-Interest, and the Foundations of Liberalism* (New York: Basic Books, 1984). For examples of the republican view, see Bernard Bailyn, *The Ideological Origins of the American Revolution* (Cambridge: Harvard University Press, 1967), Gordon Wood, *The Creation of the American Republic* (New York: W. W. Norton, 1969), and J. G. A. Pocock, *The Machiavellian Moment: Florentine Political Thought and the Atlantic Republican Tradition* (Princeton: Princeton University Press, 1975).

10. Wood, *The Creation of the American Republic*, pp. 24, 61.

largely through the preservation of boundaries between and among institutions that the rights of persons were to be secured."[11] Perhaps the most vivid constitutional expression of this fact is that the Bill of Rights did not apply to the states and was not understood to create individual immunities from all government action. When Madison proposed, in 1789, a constitutional amendment providing that "no State shall infringe the equal rights of conscience, nor the freedom of speech or of the press, nor of the right of trial by jury in criminal cases," the liberal, rights-based ethic found its clearest early expression. But Madison's proposal was rejected by the Senate, and did not succeed until the Fourteenth Amendment was passed some seventy-nine years later.

Finally, the early republic was a place where the possibility of civic virtue was a live concern. Some saw civic virtue as essential to the preservation of liberty; others despaired of virtue and sought to design institutions that could function without it.[12] But as Tocqueville found in his visit to the New England townships, public life functioned in part as an education in citizenship: "Town meetings are to liberty what primary schools are to science; they bring it within the people's reach, they teach men how to use and how to enjoy it. A nation may establish a free government, but without municipal institutions it cannot have the spirit of liberty."[13]

B. The National Republic

The transition to the national republic—and, ultimately, the procedural republic—began to unfold from the end of the Civil War to the turn of the century.[14] As national markets and large-scale

---

11. Tribe, *American Constitutional Law* (Mineola, N.Y.: The Foundation Press, 1978), pp. 2-3.

12. See, for example, Madison, *Federalist*, No. 51, ed. Jacob E. Cooke (Middletown, Conn.: Wesleyan University Press, 1961), and Herbert Storing, *What the Anti-Federalists Were For: The Political Thought of the Opponents of the Constitution* (Chicago: University of Chicago Press, 1981), chap. 3.

13. Tocqueville, *Democracy in America*, 2 vols., trans. Phillips Bradley (New York: Knopf, 1945), vol. 1, chap. 5.

14. In this and the following section, I have drawn from my article entitled "The Procedural Republic and the Unencumbered Self," *Political Theory* 12 (1984), pp. 81-96.

enterprise displaced a decentralized economy, the decentralized political forms of the early republic became outmoded as well. If democracy was to survive, the concentration of economic power would have to be met by a similar concentration of political power. But the Progressives understood—or some of them did — that the success of democracy required more than the centralization of government; it also required the nationalization of politics. The primary form of political community had to be recast on a national scale. For Herbert Croly, writing in 1909, the "nationalizing of American political, economic, and social life" was "an essentially formative and enlightening political transformation." We would become more of a democracy only as we became "more of a nation . . . in ideas, in institutions, and in spirit."[15]

This nationalizing project would be consummated in the New Deal, but for the democratic tradition in America, the embrace of the nation was a decisive departure. From Jefferson to the Populists, the party of democracy in American political debate had been, roughly speaking, the party of the provinces, of decentralized power, of small-town and small-scale America. And against them had stood the party of the nation — first Federalists, then Whigs, then the Republicans of Lincoln — a party that spoke for the consolidation of the union. It was thus the historic achievement of the New Deal to unite, in a single party and political program, what Samuel Beer has called "liberalism and the national idea."[16]

What matters for our purpose is that, in the twentieth century, liberalism made its peace with concentrated power. But it was understood at the start that the terms of this peace required a strong sense of national community, morally and politically, to underwrite the extended involvements of a modern industrial order. If a virtuous republic of small-scale, democratic communities was no longer a possibility, a national republic seemed democracy's next best hope. This was still, in principle at least, a politics of the common good. It looked to the nation not as a neutral framework for the play of competing interests, but rather

---

15. Croly, *The Promise of American Life* (Indianapolis: Bobbs-Merrill, 1965), pp. 270-73.
16. Beer, "Liberalism and the National Idea," *The Public Interest*, Fall 1966, pp. 70-82.

as a formative community, concerned to shape a common life suited to the scale of modern social and economic forms. But by the mid- or late twentieth century, the national republic had run its course. Except during extraordinary moments such as war, the nation proved too vast a scale across which to cultivate the shared self-understandings necessary to community in the formative, or constitutive, sense. And yet, given the scale of economic and political life, there seemed no turning back. If so extended a republic could not sustain a politics of the common good, a different sort of legitimating ethic would have to be found. Thus the gradual shift, in our practices and institutions, from a public philosophy of common purposes to one of fair procedures, from the national republic to the procedural republic.

C. The Procedural Republic

The procedural republic represents the triumph of a liberal public philosophy over a republican one, with adverse consequences for democratic politics and the legitimacy of the regime. It reverses the terms of relation between liberty and democracy, transforms the relation of the individual and nation-state, and tends to undercut the kind of community on which it nonetheless depends. Liberty in the procedural republic is defined not as a function of democracy but in opposition to democracy, as an individual's guarantee against what the majority might will. I am free insofar as I am the bearer of rights, where rights are trumps.[17] Unlike the liberty of the early republic, the modern version permits—in fact, even requires—concentrated power. This has at least partly to do with the universalizing logic of rights. Insofar as I have a right, whether to free speech or to a minimum income, its provision cannot be left to the vagaries of local preferences but must be assured at the most comprehensive level of political association. It cannot be one thing in New York and another in Alabama. As rights and entitlements expand, politics is therefore displaced from smaller forms of association and relocated at the most universal form—in our case,

---

17. See Ronald Dworkin, "Liberalism," in *Public and Private Morality,* ed. Stuart Hampshire (Cambridge: Cambridge University Press, 1978), p. 136.

the nation. And even as politics flows to the nation, power shifts away from democratic institutions (such as legislatures and political parties) toward institutions designed to be insulated from democratic pressures, and hence better equipped to dispense and defend individual rights (notably the judiciary and bureaucracy).

These institutional developments may begin to account for the sense of powerlessness that the welfare state fails to address and in some ways doubtless deepens. But it seems to me a further clue to our condition can be located in the vision of the unencumbered self that animates the liberal ethic. It is a striking feature of the welfare state that it offers a powerful promise of individual rights and also demands of its citizens a high measure of mutual engagement. But the self-image that attends the rights cannot sustain the engagement. As bearers of rights, where rights are trumps, we think of ourselves as freely choosing, individual selves, unbound by obligations antecedent to rights, or to the agreements we make. And yet, as citizens of the procedural republic that secures these rights, we find ourselves implicated willy-nilly in a formidable array of dependencies and expectations we did not choose and increasingly reject.

In our public life, we are more entangled, but less attached, than ever before. It is as though the unencumbered self presupposed by the liberal ethic had begun to come true—less liberated than disempowered, entangled in a network of obligations and involvements unassociated with any act of will and yet unmediated by those common identifications or expansive self-definitions that would make them tolerable. As the scale of social and political organization has become more comprehensive, the terms of our collective identity have become more fragmented, and the forms of political life have outrun the common purposes needed to sustain them.

Maritain in and on America

Ralph McInerny

We Americans are embarrassingly eager to be instructed by others, and there is ever a fresh supply of visiting pundits, condescending continentals, and ideological intelligentsia to supply our need. Nowadays the United Nations has become a running seminar where diplomats from various totalitarian and/or undeveloped societies instruct us in our duties. And we pay for the privilege. I leave it to historians to determine if there has ever been docility such as ours since the beginning of recorded time.

In earlier, more leisurely eras, a book of reminiscences on America was a mandatory addition to a visiting European's *oeuvre*—once he was safely home. Mrs. Trollope made a fortune with a book telling of her adventures among the wild Americans during her ill-fated effort to found an emporium in Cincinnati. Dickens' *American Notes* was more gentle, but still critical. He particularly disliked the spitting of tobacco juice. Anthony Trollope and Thackeray—not to mention Oscar Wilde—were more positive. In our own time, the negative British estimate of the United States has been carried on by Graham Greene.

All this by way of preface to some remarks about Jacques Maritain's reflections on America—those contained in the 1958 book of that title, and those which antedate and follow it. Maritain himself refers to Chateaubriand and Tocqueville, and we are at once put in mind of a French literary tradition whose contributions are of a much more cerebral kind. Books 6 through 8 of *Mémoires d'outre-tombe* tell of Chateaubriand's youthful visit to these shores and include his charming account of dropping

33

by Washington's house in Philadelphia and being asked to come back for dinner. His comparison of Washington and Napoléon is striking: Washington, having helped lift his country to independence, died among the universal grief of his compatriots. Napoléon robbed France of independence and died in exile; the posted notice of his death was ignored by passersby. Like Tocqueville, Chateaubriand had come here to see the future and found that it worked. What failed in France still flourished here. One gifted with a strong historical imagination can visualize the scene that met those friendly, intelligent, and aristocratic eyes. America represented a political culture which, whatever its faults, was the future.

It was perfectly fitting that Maritain should cite these predecessors—like theirs, his admiration for this country had profound roots. If democracy is the best political expression of Christianity, as Maritain held, and if democracy has achieved its highest level in the United States, as he also held, his interest had to be as intense as it was.

And yet his love for America surprised him. He had nursed the European prejudices he cites at the beginning of *Reflections on America* (1958). In *Integral Humanism* (1936), he sketched a political ideal that could only follow the liquidation of capitalism. Even so, Maritain ended up describing the America to which he responded with love. That description will serve as my text.

MARITAIN IN AMERICA

Jacques Maritain's first visit to North America was in 1933, when he was asked to give a course at the Pontifical Institute of Mediaeval Studies in Toronto. From Toronto, he went to Chicago, where he lectured on the topic of culture and liberty in English, a language he claims he did not then know. On that occasion Maritain made friendships—with Robert Hutchins, Mortimer Adler, and John U. Nef—that lasted a lifetime. Unsuccessful efforts were made to get Maritain an appointment at the University of Chicago, but he returned to give some lectures in the autumn of 1934. Maritain repeated the visits to Chicago in 1938 and 1940, when he brought with him his wife, Raissa, and Vera Oumansoff, his sister-in-law. During the early thirties, Maritain also began his connection with the University of Notre Dame, where his friend Yves Simon was to teach before joining the fac-

ulty of the University of Chicago. Waldemar Gurian, founder of
Notre Dame's *Review of Politics*, was involved in arrangements
for the course Maritain taught on social and political philosophy
in South Bend in 1938. On this occasion, Maritain's anti-Franco
stand called forth some sharp questioning, but this did not pre-
vent the beginning of a long and almost sentimental association
between him and the university. Maritain was present for the
opening of the Jacques Maritain Center in 1957; a photograph of
the then aging philosopher—flanked by Joseph Evans, the first
director of the Center, Father Leo R. Ward, C.S.C., and Frank
Keegan—commemorates the event. And he actually bequeathed
his heart to Notre Dame, although French medical laws pre-
vented this wish from being carried out.

The preceding history shows that Maritain's first encounters with the United States were in the Midwest. Nonetheless, in 1934 he spoke in New York—where, along with academic
and cultural notables, he came to know Dorothy Day and the
Catholic Worker Movement—and he lectured in Washington at
the Catholic University of America. On later visits to New York,
he met the staff of *Commonweal* (a meeting that began another
long association) and Thomas Merton. Merton and Maritain
were to be lifelong friends; among the most moving
photographs John Howard Griffin took were those of Maritain
and Merton in the latter's hermitage at Gethsemani Trappist
Abbey in Kentucky.

In January 1940, Maritain, his wife, and his sister-in-law
sailed from France for what was to be a five-year wartime exile
in the United States. The Maritains lived in New York, and
Jacques was involved in the École Libre, which was housed in
the New School. He continued to lecture at various universities
—Columbia, Princeton, Chicago, Notre Dame, Toronto—as well
as to teach courses at the École Libre. And he wrote. Late in 1944
he made a trip to France. The American sojourn ended in 1945,
when Maritain was appointed French ambassador to the
Vatican.

Three years later, Maritain was offered and accepted an appointment to Princeton University, where he taught Thomistic
moral philosophy for five years — from 1948 to 1952 — after
which he was given emeritus status. The Maritains continued to
live in Princeton until 1960. During this period Maritain continued to teach and lecture at various universities. The Walgreen

Lectures he delivered at the University of Chicago became *Man and the State*. In 1960 Maritain took his dying wife back to France. After her death, he continued to make visits to the United States, coming to lecture at the old and favored places—Notre Dame, Chicago, Toronto.

But enough. It is clear that Jacques Maritain was more than a visitor to the United States. From 1940 to 1960, except during his three-year stint as ambassador to the Vatican, he was a resident of this country. Those two decades had been preceded by many visits, and they would be followed by others. Maritain's American contacts were many and various. When he spoke of this country, then, he did so with unusual authority. What did he have to say?

MARITAIN ON AMERICA

I do not propose to present the full scope of Maritain's *Reflections on America*. For one thing, such a summary would suggest that the book itself is difficult, or large, or in need of some intermediary. It is none of these. It is a short book that speaks with immediacy to the reader, retaining the conversational tone of the three lectures Maritain gave to the Committee on Social Thought at the University of Chicago which form the basis of the book.[1] I wish only to draw your attention to one or two items of random curiosity and then to concentrate on what seems to me essential to Maritain's vision of America.

One who reads this 1958 book some thirty years later will, I think, be struck by the absence of any reference to the atomic bomb or nuclear weapons. It has become fashionable to say that our minds have been haunted by thoughts of imminent annihilation since 1945. It is nice to have one's own memories corroborated by silence on this subject in Maritain's reflections.

One is also struck by an untroubled certainty that democracy not only is the essence of America but is as well the future of the globe. Maritain gave these lectures during

---

1. We have these lectures in the Jacques Maritain Center. Maritain wrote them in his miniscule hand, almost always using pencil, on four-by-seven-inch yellow sheets. His facility with written English is apparent here, however troublesome his accent remained; the published book differs very little from these handwritten pages.

Eisenhower's second term, and quoted Adlai Stevenson in them; in a few years Kennedy's inaugural address would give eloquent voice to the country's sense of an international mission. Maritain is clearly at home with this vision. How distant we seem today from that untroubled confidence, forever reading sinister motives into the almost missionary internationalism that then characterized the two national parties.

Further, one is struck by Maritain's remarks about capitalism. Maritain notes that one of his first impressions of America was that a conflict exists between the inner logic of capitalism and the people he saw living it. What is that inner logic? "Its inner logic, as I knew it—originally grounded as it was on the principle of the fecundity of money and the absolute primacy of individual profit—was, everywhere in the world, inhuman and materialist."[2] This was the way he had envisaged capitalism in *Integral Humanism*.[3] "But by a strange paradox, the people who lived and toiled under this structure or ritual of civilization were keeping their own souls apart from it. At least as regards the essentials, their souls and vital energy, their dreams, their everyday effort, their idealism and generosity, were running against the grain of the inner logic of the superimposed structure. They were freedom-loving and mankind-loving people, people clinging to the importance of ethical standards, anxious to save the world, the most humane and the least materialist among modern peoples which had reached the industrial stage."[4] Maritain returns to this subject in his sixth chapter, "The Old Tag of American Materialism," in which he develops at some length his conviction that America is not a materialist nation. Americans may be middle class, but they are not bourgeois, not stingy, avaricious, or narrowly possessive.

Well, all that makes pretty bracing reading, and it leads to what I regard as central to Maritain's notion of what America is. If we are not materialist, are we spiritual? Not only are we that, Maritain maintains, but there is in this country a great thirst for,

---

2. Maritain, *Reflections on America* (New York: Scribner's, 1958), p. 21.

3. See Maritain, *Integral Humanism: Temporal and Spiritual Problems of a New Christendom*, trans. Joseph Evans (Notre Dame, Ind.: University of Notre Dame Press, 1973), pp. 190-92.

4. Maritain, *Reflections on America*, p. 22.

a great potential for—contemplation. He mentions the popularity of the writings of Thomas Merton. He cites his own judgment of 1938 that a small but effective turn to contemplative activity will gradually "modify the general scheme of values."[5] Characteristically, Maritain illustrates what he means by invoking American literature. "Let me only add that from *Moby Dick* and *The Scarlet Letter* to *Look Homeward, Angel* and *Requiem for a Nun*—from Edgar Allan Poe and Emily Dickinson to Hart Crane, Allen Tate and T. S. Eliot (who has remained an American in spite of himself)—American literature, in its most objectively careful scrutinies, has been preoccupied with the beyond and the nameless which haunt our blood. Man, as it sees him, is a restless being gropingly, sometimes miserably, at grips with his fleshly condition — whom obviously no kind of materialist paradise can ever satisfy."[6]

Three decades ago we were seen by this astute visitor as a people with a spiritual destiny, a people whose literature, political structures, and economy revealed this orientation to the "something more" — if not in actual fact, then in proximate potency.[7]

These last remarks occur in a section late in *Reflections* in which Maritain makes explicit reference to the views he had expressed in *Integral Humanism*. There he had put forth an ideal of society as personalist, communitarian, and pluralist.[8] That society would be not a sacral but a secular one. What, then, of religion in America? In what way can the United States manifest the following notion? "One of the main themes in *Humanisme Integral* is the notion of a temporal civilization

---

5. See Maritain, *Scholasticism and Politics* (New York: Macmillan, 1940), and *Reflections on America*, p. 41.

6. Maritain, *Reflections on America*, p. 42.

7. Maritain proclaimed, "The American economy is now growing beyond capitalism, in the proper, classical sense of this word" (*Reflections on America*, p. 178).

8. And here Maritain acknowledges what I have called second sight on his love at first sight. "The curious thing in this connection is that, fond as I may have been of America as soon as I saw her, and probably because of the particular perspective in which *Humanisme Integral* was written, it took a rather long time for me to become aware of the kind of congeniality which existed between what is going on in this country and a number of views I had expressed in my book" (*Reflections on America*, p. 175).

which is not 'sacral' but secular in nature, and in which men belonging to diverse spiritual lineages work together for the terrestrial common good, but which, for all that, is a civilization religiously inspired and vitally Christian in its concrete behavior and morality as a social body."[9] Maritain quotes an article by Peter Drucker, "Organized Religion and the American Creed," which appeared in *The Review of Politics* in July 1956. Speaking of the "establishment clause" in the First Amendment, Drucker takes it to mean that the state must neither support nor favor any one religious denomination. "But at the same time the state must always sponsor, protect, and favor religious life in general. The United States is indeed a 'secular' state as far as any one denomination is concerned. But it is at the same time a 'religious' commonwealth as concerns the general belief in the necessity of a truly religious basis of citizenship."[10] By citing this point, Maritain accepts it as a gloss on what he means by a secular as opposed to a sacral society. Moreover, he quotes the following description of the Constitution from *Man and the State:* "It can be described as an outstanding lay Christian document tinged with the philosophy of the day. The spirit and inspiration of this great political Christian document is basically repugnant to the idea of making human society stand aloof from God and from any religious faith. Thanksgiving and public prayer, the invocation of the name of God at the occasion of any major official gathering, are, in the practical behavior of the nation, a token of this same spirit and inspiration."[11] He sees the thought of the Founding Fathers— "their philosophy of life and their political philosophy, their notion of natural law and of human rights" — as permeated with concepts "worked out by Christian reason and backed up by an unshakable religious feeling."[12]

What strange reading these thoughtful remarks make just thirty years after they were spoken. I want to reflect on them in the light of recent national experience.

---

9. Maritain, *Reflections on America*, pp. 179-80.
10. Maritain, *Reflections on America*, p. 181.
11. Maritain, *Man and the State* (Chicago: University of Chicago Press, 1951), pp. 183-84; cited in *Reflections on America*, p. 182.
12. Maritain, *Reflections on America*, p. 183.

THE WIDER CONTEXT

The student of Maritain will realize that these reflections on America repose on a vast amount of writing about religion and politics in the modern state. One can speak without exaggeration of Maritain's political philosophy, but then one can also speak of his aesthetics, his philosophy of history and of science, his metaphysics, and his account of contemplation. Maritain is a philosopher in the grand manner, of the old school. He is a systematic philosopher, but not in the sense of professing a seamless whole closed in upon itself where every question has its answer; he is a Thomist, a student of Saint Thomas from the time of his conversion.[13] This inspiration — *Vae mihi si non thomistizavero*, he has exclaimed—opened his mind to the full range of practical and theoretical questions, and his published work makes it clear that he considered no part of knowledge and culture alien to him. The importance of this for understanding his political views is now clear. His ultimate perspective will be, if not overtly theological, then metaphysical, and by that I mean theistic.

The Thomist believes that man acts for an end because he is part of a teleological cosmos. Purpose is not confined to the human realm but permeates the natural world as well. This contrasts with discussions of morals and politics which assume that the natural world—and this includes the human body—is the realm of necessity, pushed from behind, not tugged forward by a goal, and that man with his projects is superimposed on this inert background. How can freedom blend with such necessity? For Maritain, the world and man have destinies: from God they come, and to God they go. If this is the case, then an atheistic account must be wrong.

This is almost precisely the opposite outlook from that which seems dominant now. The current working assumption is that our view of man and society must be godless, at most neutral toward theism, in practice antagonistic to it. The citizen who thinks his religious beliefs are relevant to political action

---

13. His general introduction to Thomas and Thomism, *The Angelic Doctor*, will be known, but of profound importance is the account Maritain gives of the *cercles d'etudes Thomistes* in *Carnet de Notes* (Paris: Desclee de Brouwer, 1965). The statutes are reprinted on pp. 396-405.

is regarded as a menace, one who would impose his private beliefs—false, of course—on his fellows. If he would function in civil society, he must become for the nonce an agnostic, a believer whose religious beliefs are irrelevant. Is not this the prominent understanding of the separation of church and state, so much so that it is espoused and preached by Catholic politicians? Is this not why we find it almost quaint for Maritain, and Peter Drucker, to say that while the state must espouse no one denomination, it must promote religion? From the latter-day point of view, Maritain's vision of the secular state looks decidedly sacral.

DEMOCRACY AS A FAITH

One of the most astonishing aspects of Maritain's political theory is the use to which he puts the Augustinian distinction between the City of God and the City of Man. What he calls a sacral society is a state or political community that smudges the difference between the two cities. This fusion was possible in times when there was a religious faith common to all citizens, but in modern times, where a diversity of faiths and, indeed, the presence of atheists within the political community are commonplace, such a sacral approach is no longer possible.

It must not be thought that Maritain regards the gradual separation of the spiritual and the temporal as a declension, as a failure of Christianity. *Au contraire.* Or at least, not quite. As he points out in *Man and the State,* this separation is a result of a "process which was in itself but a development of the Gospel distinction between the things that are Caesar's and the things that are God's—the civil society has become grounded on a common good and a common task which are of an earthly, 'temporal' or 'secular' order, and in which citizens belonging to diverse spiritual groups or lineages share equally. Religious division among men is in itself a misfortune. But it is a fact that we must willy-nilly recognize."[14] In the temporal order, however, democracy can play a role analogous to that which faith plays in the religious realm. Maritain does not hesitate to speak of "the democratic secular faith." "A genuine democracy implies a fundamental agreement between minds and wills on

14. Maritain, *Man and the State,* p. 108.

the bases of life in common; it is aware of itself and of its principles, and it must be capable of defending and promoting its own conception of social and political life; it must bear within itself a common human creed, the creed of freedom."[15] Maritain contrasts this with the bourgeois liberal democracy of the nineteenth century which imagined that it could accommodate conceptions inimical to its own foundations, that it could be *"neutral* even with regard to freedom."[16] It lacked a common good; it had no real common thought; it produced a society with no common faith. "The *faith* in question is a *civic* or *secular* faith, not a religious one."[17] Not only is this faith not a rival to religious faith, according to Maritain, but the more lively the religious faith, the more deeply would the secular faith in the democratic charter be adhered to. The reason for this is simply that democracy itself has sprung from a Christian inspiration; it is a political expression of the gospel.

Maritain is not through with the analogy. If faith, then heretics. There are, he says, political heretics who work to destroy the bases of common life—freedom and the practical secular faith expressed in the democratic charter.

I draw attention to these few facets of Chapter Five of *Man and the State* because they are clearly what underpins Maritain's views toward this country in *Reflections on America*. Those few remarks at the end of the latter work which suggest that, much to Maritain's own surprise, the United States is close to the ideal he sketched in *Integral Humanism*, are seriously meant.

Here is a sort of sorites expressing Maritain's outlook:

- Maritain was a Roman Catholic with an unshakable faith in the truth of Christianity.
- If Christianity is true, then what it says of man and human destiny is also true.
- The freedom and dignity of the person are central to the faith, and these tenets have fostered a gradual evolution of political thought and institutions in the direction of democracy.
- But democratic faith in free cooperation need not be

15. Maritain, *Man and the State*, p. 109.
16. Maritain, *Man and the State*, p. 110.
17. Maritain, *Man and the State*, p. 110.

grounded on Christian faith—the very Christian distinction between God and Caesar asserts this.

- That is why, despite the talk of the democratic faith and political heretics, Maritain considers the democratic charter to be productive of a secular rather than a sacral society.
- Moreover, despite the conflicting justifications that may be offered for the democratic charter—the democratic faith is, he holds, a matter of practical rather than theoretical agreement—there is a sense in which this does not matter. There is implicitly present in this faith its true foundation, no matter the false theories that might be constructed.
- The secular foundation of the democratic faith is natural law.

In that sequence we have, I believe, the gist of Maritain's thought about democracy. And, of course, the retort will be that natural law is every bit as problematical to the "modern mind" as Christian faith.

THE RIGHTS OF MAN

What prepared the way for Maritain's position on the democratic faith and its true foundation was his reflections on the notion of universal human rights. Chapter Four of *Man and the State* both recalls and completes his thoughts on this subject, and the lengthy title of the opening section is a statement of his fundamental thesis: *Men mutually opposed in their theoretical conceptions can come to a merely practical agreement regarding a list of human rights.* Maritain had before him not only the eighteenth-century universal declaration of human rights but also the International Declaration on Human Rights published by the United Nations in 1948. Indeed, he had been his country's delegate to the UNESCO meeting in Mexico City that had fashioned this document. How was agreement on such a list possible between governments and societies of such deeply divided ideas on man?

There is, of course, a cynical reply to that. Nor must we think Maritain is naive. Later in *Man and the State*, discussing world government, he notes that his basic Aristotelianism makes him wary of such a concept. It should also dictate wariness about international declarations on human rights. Maritain insists that the agreement is not an agreement on the basis of those rights. "It would be quite futile," he says, "to look for a common *rational justification* of these practical conclusions and these rights."[18] Nonetheless, rational justifications are necessary, indispensable, even though they are powerless to create agreement among men. "As long as there is no unity of faith or unity of philosophy in the minds of men, the interpretations and justifications will be in mutual conflict."[19] The agreement, he maintains, is practical, even pragmatic, rather than theoretical.

Maritain holds that there is one true theoretical or philosophical foundation of human rights and that others are false or woefully inadequate. He thinks that if others have a theoretical or philosophical foundation that is in conflict with his own, theirs is false. Yet, from a practical point of view, this does not matter.

Surely this is a curious position, and if this were all there is to it, the obvious retort would be that the agreement Maritain speaks of is, at most, verbal. If "freedom of expression" and "freedom to emigrate" mean quite different things in different societies, what is the value of "agreeing" on freedom of expression and freedom to emigrate? Unless Maritain can maintain that in some fundamental sense those who disagree are in agreement—and not merely in what he calls practical agreement— his position must seem cynical. But of course natural law is a justification which includes the claim that everyone has the wherewithal right now to see the truth of that justification. This is the point of introducing here his distinction between the ontological natural law and the gnoseological natural law, the former being the real basis for the latter recognition. The theory of natural law maintains that even those who reject it are accepting it, at least to some degree, and the degree to which they accept it is the seed of theoretical and not merely practical agreement. The ontological natural law is, therefore, the implicit and often unrecognized basis for the kind of practical agreement Maritain speaks of, and it can also ground an articulated agreement when the ground (the ontological) is known (the gnoseological). As Saint Thomas insisted, it is very much like saying

18. Maritain, *Man and the State,* p. 76.
19. Maritain, *Man and the State,* p. 79.

that one who denies the principle of contradiction must invoke it; so, too, one who denies the precepts of natural law nonetheless implicitly honors them.[20]

CONCLUSION

Jacques Maritain joins a long list of Frenchmen who saw beneath the surface roughness of this country, beneath its flaws and imperfections, a universal human ideal being realized. When his earlier more or less standard anti-Americanism and anti-capitalism evaporated because of his lengthy sojourn here, he did not need to concoct a new theory to explain his affection and respect for the United States. Rather, it seemed to him that, although he had not suspected it before, this country best exemplified a democratic ideal he had been trying to formulate earlier. His experience here did not generate a new theory. Rather, familiarity with America led him to think that it met the specifications of a theory he had already formed. This is not said to diminish the very real love he felt for America. Who has not felt that his beloved assumes a waiting role even as she shapes and alters it?

---

20. See *Summa theologiae,* IaIIae, q. 94, a. 2, as well as my *Ethica Thomistica: The Moral Philosophy of Thomas Aquinas* (Washington: Catholic University of America Press, 1984).

The Story of an Encounter

Paul T. Stallsworth

The two-day conference titled "Moral Possibilities, Moral Limitations in the Right Ordering of the World" could not be tagged as an unambitious undertaking. Seated around the conference table in Room 405 of The Princeton Club of New York, the twenty-five scholarly participants appeared quite eager to delve into the almost cosmic subject at hand. That meant they were especially anxious to discuss the principal theme of the conference: Reinhold Niebuhr—his life, his work, and his relevance.

As is his custom as conference moderator, Richard John Neuhaus, Director of The Rockford Institute Center on Religion and Society, welcomed the conferees and then issued a warning: "In my moderating style I oscillate between Genghis Khan and Carl Rogers." Thankfully, during most of the conference Neuhaus came across as a gentlemanly Genghis Khan and/or a Carl Rogers with some directive backbone. In fact, his first directive was to order the presentation of the five conference papers. The paper on Niebuhr and his contemporary relevance by Richard Wightman Fox was to be discussed first, followed by the papers by Michael J. Sandel and Ralph McInerny. The papers by Stanley Hauerwas and Robin W. Lovin would be considered in tandem during the final session of the conference.

NIEBUHR AND NOW

Richard Fox, who teaches history at Reed College, was the first presenter to take the floor. He started the conference thinking about Reinhold Niebuhr the man: "I've often wondered what Reinhold Niebuhr would have been like in a group such as ours. I've often been told that he took immediate possession of a room like this. There was something charismatic, something overwhelming about his presence. I've often wondered whether that was attributable to Niebuhr's personality or to the time in which he lived, which was receptive to those who embodied masculine authority."

Then Fox used an anecdote as evidence of Niebuhr's powerful presence: "I'm reminded of a story that Roland Bainton told me in an interview. He, like Niebuhr, was a member of something called the Younger Theologians, which got going in the 1930s with H. Richard Niebuhr and various other well-known theologians on the East Coast. Bainton was sitting next to Richard Niebuhr during one of the meetings of this group. Reinhold was of course sitting at the table like everybody else, but he was very agitated. He kept climbing out of his seat; he found it very hard to sit and take in what other people were saying. He wanted to be speaking even when he was listening. So Reinhold was almost mounting the table in excitement, trying to respond to something someone was saying. At this point, so the story goes, Richard Niebuhr leaned over to Bainton and said, 'I don't think Jesus ever got quite that agitated.' I think this says something about both Niebuhr and the time in which he lived—that he was able to assume this incredible authority at whatever gathering he attended. It could be a small group, a classroom of several hundred students, or a big meeting of the ADA with thousands in the audience. Whatever the setting, he had the ability to take possession of the gathering."

Paul Ramsey, who at the time of the conference was at the Center of Theological Inquiry and who himself had been a veritable center of theological inquiry for years, was not entirely satisfied with Fox's little story about Niebuhr's impatience. "Bainton may remember that particular occasion correctly," he conceded, "but it would have been atypical: in those days theologians engaged in civil discourse." For example, he continued, if a member of the Younger Theologians rambled on for twenty minutes at a meeting, everybody present listened politely. And even "when Reinnie thought pious sentimentalities were being expressed, he did not jump out of his seat. He took out his paper and, instead of doodling, started working on his next Sunday sermon."

Another who knew Niebuhr, Roger Shinn of Union Theological Seminary in New York, resisted Fox's portrait of a domineering Niebuhr. "It is quite true that Niebuhr had the ability—and often used it—to galvanize a group, to become the focus of the discussion. But it is also true that he was very able to listen quietly and meditatively, sometimes making notes for the future. I recall in particular a two-year faculty seminar at Columbia University that Niebuhr attended; a couple of doctoral students, myself included, were allowed to sit in. It was a seminar on political theory and practice chaired by Salo Baron —and Niebuhr had an almost reverential admiration for Baron's historical scholarship. At that seminar Niebuhr was simply one of the group. Not surprisingly, on the night he presented his paper, he took off in his characteristic way. But at other times he listened, chimed in, and commented in the way that others did, recognizing that many people there knew a great deal that he did not. He never undertook to correct Baron on Jewish history, or political scientists on their area of expertise.

"I particularly remember the occasion when I addressed a meeting of the Fellowship of Socialist Christians, just about the time it changed to the Frontier Fellowship. Niebuhr was in the audience. But, although he questioned me and offered some comments, there was not the slightest doubt that I, a student, was the center of the group."

Earlier Fox had raised a question about Niebuhr's inclinations to be a friend and a family man. Charles Brown, a Marguerite Eyer Wilbur Fellow who lives close to Niebuhr's birthplace—Wright City, Missouri—came to Niebuhr's defense: "Harvey Cox wrote an article that hinges mainly on Niebuhr's relationship with Charles C. Morrison and Waldo Frank. Niebuhr told Frank that he was too busy to spend as much time with him as Frank wanted. It seems to me that it was Frank's role as a friend to understand this constraint, since Niebuhr was a busy man. Niebuhr had set aside some time for Frank, but there were times when he was simply too busy to see him. As for Morrison, we all know that Niebuhr broke with Morrison on the pacifist issue on the eve of World War II; there was a breach of friendship. Yet Niebuhr remained friends with other people with whom he had deep differences. Niebuhr's relationship with the pacifist Lynn Harold Hough, whom Niebuhr had met in Detroit, is an example. Hough and Niebuhr remained friends when Hough was Dean at Drew. In fact, Reinhold and Ursula visited Hough and his wife a number of times there. In 1940 Hough went around giving speeches advocating that the United States lay down its arms so that the Germans might love Americans. From Niebuhr's point of view, this was terribly naive, but he remained Hough's friend."

Furthermore, Brown argued, Niebuhr's views on family life were quite remarkable. For proof he read aloud a paragraph that Niebuhr had penned in 1959: "In the relation between husband and wife, the modern family stands under the obvious necessity of constantly reassessing the position of the woman in the home and the community because many factors in secular civilization have given her a potential freedom and equality which were not granted in an agrarian civilization and which cannot be denied now."

Fox, unpersuaded by Brown, offered this rejoinder: "It simply isn't true that Hough and Niebuhr remained close friends. If you talk to Ursula about it, she will tell you that Hough was a buffoon. In fact, Reinhold wrote letters in which he referred to Hough as a fool. The important point is that Niebuhr did subordinate the cultivation of friendship to other goods and virtues. He didn't regard friendship as a major preoccupation of his daily life. He was always too busy for friendships; he didn't linger and cultivate them.

"One can also see these priorities in his family life. He was very rarely at home, not as much as his family might have wished, particularly before his stroke. It tells us a lot about the masculine, patriarchal authority structure of this earlier period. Despite what he wrote in 1959, it is clear that he subordinated family relationships as well as friendships to public enterprises."

Believing a little clarity of definition is always in order, Ramsey spoke up: "C. S. Lewis has given us a great definition of friendship: friends are friends around a common cause. They do not look eye to eye like lovers do. The relationship is not I-thou; it is something suddenly found in congeniality. We just don't cultivate friendship as such, and there are times when friendships do come to an end, when friendship is understood in this way."

Once again Roger Shinn defended his former colleague at

Union. First, Shinn addressed Fox: "I feel compelled to come back to the issue of friendship. I have a point to make about Harvey Cox. You cited him in your paper, Professor Fox, but he doesn't help you at all, because Cox's only evidence is your book, so he's only playing back your own ideas to you."

Shinn continued, "When Niebuhr was a teacher at Union, until his illness, if you asked students who they thought was their best friend on the faculty, more would have named Niebuhr than anyone else.

"All of us can say to some people with whom we are arguing, 'This argument does not affect our friendship.' But with others it does. You come to Mannheim's point: in ideological argument there is a juncture at which argument inevitably becomes an assault on character. We don't like it, but that's the case. I couldn't say to a Hitler or a Stalin, 'I'm sure you're a good person, though I disagree with the way you work things out.' There comes a point in ideological argument when you reject the other person's character. That's what happened with Niebuhr and Morrison. I wish the rift could have been more graceful, but it's there. The other case was Waldo Frank. I can think of a lot of people who have not had as much time for me as I have wanted, and I know people who say I haven't had as much time for them as they have wanted. This is part of human finitude."

Niebuhr's family life was the next item on Shinn's agenda: "In a period when the phenomenon of two-career couples was much less common than it is now, Reinhold and Ursula were both professionals with full-time jobs. They were trying to work that out, just as my daughters and their spouses are trying to work it out now. It was and is hard to do. Reinhold spent much time in the kitchen. Ursula was the boss in the kitchen, but Reinhold was there in a way that Tillich certainly was not."

At this point Neuhaus interjected a comment: "As I understand it, Paul Tillich was in the kitchen a lot too." The laughter that followed, it is hoped, did not signal approval of the various ways in which Tillich was in the kitchen.

Shinn continued by noting that Hannah Tillich had once said to Ursula, "I had no idea what a hard life you had." Ursula commented later, "All I could think of to say was that I didn't know that I had had a hard life."

Shinn then interpreted Ursula's reply: "I do think Ursula's

life was hard during Reinhold's illness. At that point, out of wife-
ly affection, she subordinated her career to look after him. Prior
to that, all of the assumptions that all of us had about the male
being the main professional in the family and so on were, I'm
sure, a part of that family. But they adjusted more than most
families of their era to the challenges of a two-career couple."

Fox remained unconvinced by this rebuttal, and he made a
final adamant point: "The assumption of Niebuhr's adult life was
that he had work to do in the public realm and that that came
first. That came before family in a very identifiable way, as Ursula has confirmed. When Reinhold was at home, granted, he did
the dishes. But, whatever the sharing around the kitchen might
have been, he simply wasn't around the kitchen very much."

Niebuhrian Orthodoxy

The issue of Reinhold Niebuhr's theology surfaced very early in
the conference and remained on the surface throughout. Richard
Fox was the first to bring it up: "For Niebuhr, the Bible was a
symbolic organ. It was something that someone could appeal to
for wisdom. It was not something that was the starting point of
reflection. The starting point of reflection was experience."

Wait a minute—let's be clear about what we mean by "experience," urged Ralph McInerny of the University of Notre
Dame.

Fox responded immediately: "Niebuhr was not troubled
by hermeneutical issues. For example, he thought that he expe-
rienced original sin in everyday life. He thought that all things
human, given enough time, would go badly. He thought that his
own experience of the communist movement in the 1930s
showed that original sin was a social as well as an individual
fact. Therefore, the Bible and its understanding of original sin
are true, because they were congruent with and in accordance
with his experience. In this respect his theology grows out of his
ethics, politics, and experience. His theology is not reducible to
such, but I do think his theology is dependent upon them. To
Niebuhr, theology was reflection upon practical experience, not
reflection upon the biblical tradition itself."

Roger Shinn strongly urged that Niebuhr's theology did
not live by experience alone: "Gustavo Gutiérrez's definition of
theology fits Niebuhr rather well—'Theology is critical reflec-

tion on praxis in the light of the Word.' If you leave out 'in the light of the Word,' the description is incomplete. Niebuhr never tried to meet an argument by saying, 'The Bible says . . .' He met it by pointing to how people behave and how people feel. Niebuhr described sin in such a way that people recognized themselves as being in sin. On the other hand, he often referred to a biblical point of view—that is, experience in the light of the Bible. In other words, he was not simply offering a generalization based on experience. After all, there is no nonideological reading of experience. There is no simple, objective report of experience. So when Niebuhr speaks of experience it is experience as interpreted in the belief that this interpretation might not be drawn out of experience without a scripture and a tradition."

Emory University's Theodore Weber reinforced Shinn's point by reminding the group that in 1939 Dietrich Bonhoeffer wrote that Reinhold Niebuhr was doing a theology of the cross —and that is quite different from doing a theology of pure experience.

"If one is going to talk about Reinhold Niebuhr and his use of experience," added Robin Lovin of the University of Chicago, "one has to retain a very broad notion of what is involved."

Stanley Hauerwas of the Divinity School at Duke agreed —partially: "That is true sometimes. At other times all Niebuhr meant by 'experience' was what he had learned."

Then Hauerwas added a personal gloss: "I should say— more as a United Methodist than as a liberal—that I gave up on the word 'experience' a long time ago. It's something that I don't want to have." Amid the laughter someone asked if that violated the Wesleyan quadrilateral—the sides of which are the Bible, church tradition, reason, and experience—for discerning Christian truth. Hauerwas, in a moment of stubbornness and perhaps overstatement, said he didn't care if it did.

Dr. David Novak, a professor at the Jewish Theological Seminary of America, worried about a certain drift he noted in Fox's paper: "One gets the impression from Fox's paper that Niebuhr was basically someone who had worked out a pragmatic social ethic and was constantly trying to catch up theologically. In other words, it seems he is being accused of being an ignorant country bumpkin, somebody who really didn't know the theological tradition very well and really wasn't sophisticated, so he had to write *The Nature and Destiny of Man* to prove

that he was a big-league theologian. I don't think that's true.
Niebuhr made an effort to work out a dialectic between his
ethics and his theology. Neither was deduced from the other.
Thus, when he wrote *The Nature and Destiny of Man*, he did so to
provide theological grounding in a true sense — not rationalization — for many of the things that he had been saying
theretofore."

Niebuhr's theology, claimed John Cooper of Bridgewater
College, and now of the Ethics and Public Policy Center, evi-
denced "an increasing understanding of natural-law theory,
particularly as defined in a very dynamic sense in the Catholic
tradition. In fact, if Niebuhr were here today, he would be interested in learning more from Catholics, in articulating a Protestant version of natural-law theory, and in challenging those
whom we might call the 're-sectarianizers' in American Protestantism."

John Hittinger of the College of St. Francis disagreed: "I
can't see Niebuhr as an advocate of natural law. I don't think he
saw nature as having definite finalities. Furthermore, he
wouldn't go along with the specific recommendations of
Catholic natural law because he had a dynamic or indeterminate
view of human nature."

Hittinger's critique was seconded and deepened by William Lazareth—theologian, former pastor of New York's Holy
Trinity Lutheran Church, and now a bishop in the Evangelical
Lutheran Church in America: "In the classroom Niebuhr, under
natural law, always taught unnatural law. For him, in other
words, law is predicated on sin. This differs from the Roman
Catholic orientation, which sees law as predicated on humanity
created in the image of God. Structurally, however, law func-
tions in exactly the same way: it protects the organic nature of
life under the sovereignty of God."

On this subject Paul Ramsey issued an unusual word: "The
publication of the first Kinsey Report had a terrific influence on
this nation. What a dull book! But Niebuhr wrote the best review
of it at the time. In it he referred to certain things that are fundamental in the nature of human beings that the entire report,
despite its enormous influence on this culture, totally ignored.
But we can't, on this basis, make Niebuhr buy into an elabora-
tion of an ontological natural law."

Lazareth then steered the discussion of Niebuhr's theology toward the more reformed idea of the sovereignty of God. But first he paused to judge Niebuhr's theology by the standards of orthodoxy: "Niebuhr was very unorthodox. He claimed to be grounded in the Christian faith, but certainly he was not Trinitarian. He had an eschatological ground for understanding the Christ event, but he completely lacked a doctrine of the Holy Spirit and the church. That left him with a great affinity for understanding the Word primarily in terms of the Hebrew Scripture's prophetic critique of challenges to God's sovereignty."

Lazareth went on to praise Niebuhr's theological project and its positive public ramifications: "The sovereignty of God is something from Niebuhr's Calvinist tradition that has permanent value in terms of relating to enlightened self-interest, civil righteousness, natural law, common grace—whatever you call it. There's something between all of us that goes beyond either me-and-my-body, me-and-my-reason, or me-and-my-Jesus that Niebuhr can help us recapture.

"The church's recapturing a sense of the God who governs all of us in a pluralistic society—regardless of our particular understanding of salvation—ought to be the way we regalvanize ourselves around a Niebuhrian contribution. In Niebuhr we have an authentic note on the insistence that the public sector need not be controlled by the church and yet still is accountable to God, regardless of our differences on how people are saved. Niebuhr recognized that life is more than simply sociologically determined and psychologically conditioned knee jerks. He has made a permanent contribution in this regard."

The Question of Liberalism

Some people make a living by coming up with categories and then sentencing others to them. One of the most popular categories of all—in terms of usage, not necessarily in terms of favor—is liberalism. That category and whether or not Niebuhr fit into it became very important to the conference conversation.

Richard Fox referred to liberalism in his opening remarks: "In my paper I suggested that the liberal consensus has broken down, that liberals on the whole have given up their faith in the state as the guarantor of justice. But I should have been more careful there, not so one-sided, because there are a lot of liberals left. I think of 'Left' liberals like Michael Harrington, Irving Howe, Francis Fox Piven, and so on. These are people who think that the real issue for the Left and for liberals today is to extend and expand the welfare state, to try to perfect the New Deal synthesis. But I see this group and its tendency as very much on the defensive and in decline and disarray." Accordingly, Fox said, he placed his hope for a reconstructed liberal consensus in a synthesis of the communitarianism of the Bellah bunch (as sketched in *Habits of the Heart*) and Niebuhr's cold political realism.

To this Paul Ramsey replied, "I'd like to make two suggestions. First, it would be very helpful if everyone who uses the term 'liberalism' would explain what he means by it. Second, it would help me if everyone who speaks of Niebuhr as a liberal could tell me what he thinks Niebuhr understood liberalism to be."

The first to respond to Ramsey was Roger Shinn: "Without defining what a liberal is, I want to recall an incident in 1959, Niebuhr's last year at Union. I wandered into his office, which was next door to mine. He had just received some hate mail in response to some public criticisms he had made of Billy Graham. He said that he hadn't realized how much of this kind of animosity was out there. In Morningside Heights he was a critic of liberalism; in other contexts he was a liberal of liberals. So I commented rather brashly, 'Reinnie, I always said that you were more of a liberal than you thought you were.' With his usual generosity, he said, 'Of course, you were right. You were right.'"

John Cooper then bravely attempted a definition: "What I mean by 'liberalism' — at least as I try to apply that term to Niebuhr — is something with an emphasis on the communitarian ideal that is informed by the American experience. It's something like a Protestant natural-law theory." Cooper added a rather controversial footnote by contending that "there is some purpose in claiming Reinhold Niebuhr as the first neoconservative because he is Calvinist, antisectarian, and conversionist with regard to the relationship between religion and culture."

By this time Richard Neuhaus had discerned a little maneuvering going on. First Richard Fox had claimed Niebuhr for a reborn liberalism. Now John Cooper was arguing that it was plausible to see Niebuhr as the first neoconservative. Neuhaus thought that these and other efforts to claim Niebuhr might be a result of our fragmented time, in which most camps are grabbing for points of reference. As the several camps grab for Niebuhr, he emerges—apart from his actual work—as the grand figure in American religion.

But that comment didn't answer the question about liberalism. And to that Marquette's Christopher Wolfe returned the conference: "There are prerequisites or conditions of liberalism—especially the authority of the state, the paternalistic family, and epistemological realism. But if you walked up to your average street-corner academic and asked what political thought is most congenial with the authority of the state, the paternalistic family, and epistemological realism, 'liberalism' probably wouldn't come to his lips. This is a striking indication of the fact that successful liberalism has always been successful partly because it is not completely liberal. The tradition of liberalism has survived partially because it has maintained elements of preliberal society that somehow have balanced it and made it able to survive. The striking thing today is that the major thrust of the philosophy of law is to try to purge liberalism of its nonliberal elements—to purify it, so to speak. That is the most self-destructive enterprise one can imagine." Taking the case of the paternalistic family, Wolfe explained that the authority of the father exists in real tension with liberalism, because liberalism elevates freedom above everything else.

Stanley Hauerwas added, "It isn't just the authority of the father that's at issue for liberalism. It's the authority of an institution, the family, into which you were born, with moral patterns that you are to be faithful to whether you have chosen them or not. The family is non-elective."

Wolfe concluded, "So you have these nonliberal elements in liberalism that have helped maintain it over time by providing a framework or structure that limits the danger of unlimited demands from liberty and equality. The question today is how to hang on to them, or resurrect them, or re-establish them."

Ramsey, who had earlier called for a definition of liberalism, now offered a twofold version: "When he was castigating liberalism, Niebuhr was castigating a classical view of economic liberalism in the political order. That is what he meant to disavow. On the other hand, I hold that Niebuhr very often used the word 'liberalism' as the equivalent of 'utopianism.'"

William Lee Miller of the University of Virginia issued a protest of sorts: "It seems to me once again that the use of the

word 'liberalism' is hopeless. Hopeless! It really does lead more
to confusion than to clarity. I think there's a shell game involved
—though not consciously—in using the word 'liberal.' There's
the rhetoric of bait and switch involved in what you mean by
'liberalism' and in whom it is you're condemning it, since everybody condemns liberalism. That would take some uncovering.
We've heard it said that Niebuhr was a liberal because he was a
communitarian. But lots of people set communitarianism over
against liberalism."

Miller went on to contend that "Reinhold Niebuhr was not
a liberal in any sense in which that word is used except in the
narrowest sense used in the newspapers. In no other meaningful sense was Niebuhr a liberal. If freedom is the first value for
a liberal, remember that Niebuhr was always setting that over
against something and being dialectical about it and recognizing that freedom is a value for community. Furthermore, if
liberalism is a picture of the individual prior to society, if
liberalism is a rudimentary Lockeanism, if liberalism is the
protection of the freedom of the individual from the social structures of society, then Niebuhr was not a liberal." Indeed, Miller
continued, Niebuhr was a critic of Locke, contract theory, and
libertarianism. He was "an American social democrat who ex-
hibited strong cultural-political-philosophical elements of con-
servatism. And, speaking of political philosophy, we see a distinctive combination in Niebuhr. We don't have many
conventional terms to describe political philosophy, so we stick
'neo' in front of the ones we do have. To use any one of these
terms to describe a dialectical thinker like Niebuhr is going to
be misleading."

Richard Fox countered, "By the 1950s Niebuhr would have
been relatively comfortable calling himself a liberal." Philosophi-
cally and theologically, Fox claimed, Niebuhr's liberalism rested
on the major role played by experience. "Politically, Niebuhr was
a liberal in an obvious and direct sense because of his reliance on
the state as the guarantor of justice. Furthermore, because he assumed the state would be goaded into action through prophetic
critique, he dispensed with a Bellah-MacIntyre approach to virtue. There is no need for a slowly growing virtue in the citizenry
if you have the state to appeal to prophetically. However,
Niebuhr was not a simple endorser of the state: he was critical of
it even though he ultimately relied on it."

At this point Fox put in a plug for his favorite kind of liberalism: "Both Bellah and Niebuhr are very centrally aware of the dangers of a consumer culture. This is especially important in the early Niebuhr, and it's the part of Niebuhr to which 'Left' liberals find themselves drawn most significantly. It is to the antitotalitarian Niebuhr that neoconservatives find themselves drawn. That's the Niebuhr of the 1950s. The earlier Niebuhr should be the Niebuhr of choice as we reflect on how to criticize and perhaps transform American society today."

Since Fox seemed to be suggesting that liberalism is one of the most elastic words in the English language, Neuhaus kidded him: "You like the word 'liberalism' for all of the reasons that Bill Miller thinks it isn't useful." Even Fox and Miller chuckled at that.

Fox completed his sketch of his favored version of liberalism with a bibliographic note: "Bellah's *Habits of the Heart* is at its best when it describes consumer culture. Likewise, Pastor Neuhaus's *Naked Public Square* is good at showing how the churches themselves have perhaps inadvertently slipped much too far into the therapeutic enterprise."

At this juncture Stanley Hauerwas called Reinhold Niebuhr a liberal and then launched into a radical critique of both Niebuhr and liberalism. "What I think is important is how one locates oneself within a history. In that sense Niebuhr is a determinative liberal, insofar as we all are. Even Burke is a liberal. Because when you start appealing to tradition qua tradition as what is politically significant, as a resource, you have already accepted a liberal perspective. Because then what is important is that you have a tradition, not what the tradition is about.

"At times Niebuhr thought that he wasn't a liberal because he was criticizing Marxism, liberalism's utopian form. But at the same time, he maintained himself steadily within the history of liberalism. He didn't even know the alternatives. The kind of Aristotelian account that would have been a genuine alternative simply was not operative for Reinhold Niebuhr. It never occurred to him because he was committed to liberalism's project. He was committed to the task of giving an account of a relatively decent government without relatively decent people. That is fundamentally a liberal project." For Niebuhr, Hauerwas added, the social order's training of people in the good was not an option because that always seemed to be a totalitarian project.

A bit puzzled, Paul Ramsey asked Hauerwas, "Now what do you mean by 'the liberal agenda'?"

Hauerwas gave it a second try: "Liberalism involves the locating of oneself in the history of political thought that is spawned predominantly after the Enlightenment. It tries to understand forms of social cooperation in a such way that people of virtue are not necessary for the proper maintenance of society and government."

Ramsey objected: "Niebuhr wasn't that sort of liberal—not the kind who would embrace those last phrases. When you add that virtuous people are unnecessary to a properly functioning society and when you make Niebuhr out to be a liberal who is not concerned with virtue, you don't have a case."

Of course, Hauerwas replied, Niebuhr presumed the ethos of liberal Protestantism, and that included virtue. Indeed, Hauerwas continued, "you can find passages in his works where he can sound as moralistic as Jerry Falwell about these matters. But when he turns to his account of the kind of people he wants to be political actors, what he wants you to understand is that behind every moral commitment lies an interest. That interest is necessary to provide a nontotalitarian form of social order." Therefore, Hauerwas was saying, although Niebuhr was an inconsistent liberal, he was still very much a liberal.

After listening to the numerous comments on liberalism from the various participants, Charles Brown tried to straighten the group out: "When Niebuhr castigated liberalism, he was criticizing the secular version of John Dewey—and especially the notion of human goodness and inevitable historical progress. On the other hand, he was certainly a liberal in the sense that he came to endorse the New Deal tradition of social policy in the interest of domestic justice."

It was difficult to tell whether the conferees were convinced by Brown's intervention or had said everything they wanted to say about Niebuhr and liberalism. For whatever reason, the issue rested.

Niebuhr for Today?

Richard Fox was the first to reply to the question of Niebuhr's contemporary relevance. He began, "People today want to know what Reinhold Niebuhr would have thought about a par-

ticular issue. Often I try to give my best guess, but I try also to
divert such queries and suggest that maybe they aren't the most
important kinds of questions to ask about Niebuhr and his
relevance today. The most important question may get at a more
general level of understanding his overall perspective on
religion and politics, not what his view would be on a particular
issue. I really want to resurrect Niebuhr, but I think it's important to let him die first. We can't assume that he's one of us, living
in our midst." After all, Fox suggested, Reinhold Niebuhr was
very much a man of the 1940s in terms of the issues he faced
(particularly the labor movement and the changes that Germany
and England underwent between 1930 and 1940), the ideas he
engaged, the perspectives he adopted and opposed, and the
identities he assumed.

Furthermore, said Fox, the 1940s are not the 1980s. "In the
1940s and beyond there was an authority structure in private life
that was based on the male-dominated family. This undergirded
the activities and debates that one found in Niebuhr's public
sphere. There was a kind of consensus on the private realm as a
realm of value, and this undergirded and made possible debates
and conflicts in the public realm. The opportunity to disagree in
public was based on a fundamental agreement in private.

"It is that private agreement which is fragmenting,
atrophying, and giving way in the 1980s," said Fox. "This makes
the public sphere an entirely different place than it was a generation ago. It may even be that the public sphere is, in Marshall
McLuhan's terms, a 'hotter place' today as people try to use it
to embody values that can no longer be safely assumed to reside
securely in the private realm. Once it was possible to consider
the public realm as a secular place, a place where one did not try
to enact values, because one had a secure realm for values in the
private sphere. Niebuhr was very much a part of this earlier
authority structure in which there was a consensus on a basically value-free public realm. These are very different times: today
there is a desperate clamoring to embody value in the public
sphere because we aren't too sure that it exists anyplace."

Paul Ramsey was ready with a comment: "I am unpersuaded, Professor Fox, by what you say about the private and
the public sphere. I remember Niebuhr saying that if he were to
retitle *Moral Man and Immoral Society,* he would call it *Not-So-
Moral Man and His More-Immoral Society.* So he certainly was

aware of the need for compromises in the midst of encounters of egos with egos, even in the family structure." Niebuhr, according to Ramsey, did not in fact assume the simple consensus on private life that Fox was describing.

After Robin Lovin claimed that Niebuhr relied less on the moral-cultural consensus than some of his contemporaries, Theodore Weber spoke. "In many respects Niebuhr was a man of his time: he was identified with labor movements and with strong opposition to communism in international politics. It is also true—witness the fact that we are here—that people keep discovering Reinhold Niebuhr and finding reasons for remembering him. That has to do less with his particular associations during his time than with his principal critique, which is often a self-critique.

"In 1952," Weber continued, "I heard Niebuhr informally address a group of pastors at Southern Methodist University. One thing that I remember from that occasion was his comment that the time may be coming when in the name of justice we may have to oppose the same labor leaders for whom our hearts bled twenty years ago. In later years I came to realize that what was operating in his mind was not simply a kind of pragmatic recognition of what was going on but his critique of the maldistribution of power. That is a fundamental element in Niebuhr's argumentation and criticism, at least from the early 1930s and probably before that. It is one of the central points in his criticism of capitalism in the 1930s and thereafter. As long as he talked about capitalism, he always had in mind the maldistribution of power. It was one of the things that kept him from being a full-scale Marxist in 1932 when he wrote *Moral Man and Immoral Society*. It is the first point in his argument about why communism is evil: the problem is the maldistribution of power. One could recite issues almost endlessly to illustrate the point."

In the world according to Niebuhr, said Weber, "there were no pure options. Any group that took power was running a very certain risk of building up its power in such a way as to try to put itself beyond questioning, and therefore create a maldistribution of power that would be unjust. This applies even to neoconservative, liberal, and liberation theologies. The issue is the balance of power."

Niebuhr's contemporary relevance, Weber went on, is based upon his balance-of-power analysis as well as his critiques of self-deception and messianism in foreign policy. These three facets of his thought keep Niebuhr from being just another "cold warrior." He remains a thinker that must be dealt with— even feminist theologians know that. "The feminists do not want to appropriate him," Weber continued, "but they do see that the big daddy is there. They have to deal with him. What is evident is an ambivalence toward the father figure—you have to kill him off but, on the other hand, there is something there that you love."

Stanley Hauerwas objected: "That's not right. As feminists have pointed out, the reason they reject Niebuhr is his strong motif of self-sacrifice. That strikes at the heart of feminist theology."

George Weigel of The James Madison Foundation then intervened to commend the Niebuhr project: "There are multiple themes in Niebuhr that have an enduring quality and that are recognized on both sides of the conventional barricades today. The sovereignty of God is one. The perdurance of irony, tragedy, and pathos is another. No matter how hard we try, these seem to be built into the structures of being human in this kind of world. Human striving has its limitations, but we need to keep trying. The necessity of self-critical patriotism — with an emphasis on both adjective and noun — is another enduring Niebuhrian theme. Principled antitotalitarianism is another. The penultimacy of the political is yet another."

Weigel admitted that "all of these themes don't seem to add up to a systematic framework like the one you find in John Courtney Murray. But what you get in Niebuhr is a sensibility. Everyone who tries to think seriously about public problems should have a Niebuhrian corner in his brain." And that sensibility, said Weigel, is most definitely related to religion, for most secular thinkers tend to lack even vague notions of irony, tragedy, and pathos.

It was then that Charles Brown listed several social-political issues which Niebuhr addressed that have proven to be perduring problems: "In 1932 Niebuhr predicted that communism would win its victories in the agrarian Orient and not in the industrial West. Lo and behold, that's what happened in China and Indochina. In 1950 he thought we would do well to write off Indochina and that the best we could hope for there was the emergence of Titoism. Again, that's about what happened."

Brown also noted the many articles that Niebuhr wrote on issues that endure—articles on the Third World, on toning down
American anti-Soviet polemics, on ecological problems, and on
the inability of economics to solve social problems.

To this Neuhaus added, "Niebuhr may have been a great
deal more prescient than Richard Fox suggests."

Fox responded by correcting Brown: "Mr. Brown's tendency to find trees out there is laudatory, but I think he's missing
the forest. The sixty articles that Niebuhr wrote on the Third
World, for example, need to be put in the context of the hundreds
of articles he wrote on Europe and other issues of his time. Furthermore, Brown's approach begs the question of the quality of
the short pieces on Asia and Vietnam. It also neglects the serious
proposal that Niebuhr made on more than one occasion that all
anticommunist warriors in Vietnam ought to be shipped over to
Thailand .and that this would somehow solve America's
problem and allow America to leave Vietnam and save face. He
made this statement publicly. He made it in print. It shows an
egregious ignorance of Asian realities, and it reveals the extent
to which Niebuhr was Eurocentric."

Fox brought up another reason to bolster his belief that
Niebuhr is relevant today in only a limited sense: "In her critique of my biography of Niebuhr in *Christianity and Crisis*,
Beverly Harrison argues that Niebuhr is part of the problem because of his male perspective and that my book is part of the
problem because of its male perspective. I think she's on to
something there. I think that Niebuhr is anachronistic in the
sense that he upholds a masculine authority structure at a time
when it cannot be upheld."

The lone woman in the room, Sidney Callahan of Mercy
College, was not so sure. "Look around!" she kidded Fox.

Everyone but Fox seemed to be laughing. "But maybe
we're superfluous," he conjectured.

Neuhaus then interpreted the dialogue: "This is an important exchange. What could it conceivably mean to say that the
people represented in this room—including their institutions
and circles of influence and stature—are superfluous to the for-
mation of religious and cultural thought in American life? Could
it be that Professor Fox's definition of cultural change is very
much attuned to a very particular, class-specifiable, elitist definition of American reality? Fox understands Ms. Harrison's

review, for example, as something that he is obligated to respond to. I—along with others in this room—would be quite prepared to say that Professor Fox shouldn't feel any such obligation at all. And I would say so without a scintilla of suspicion that that makes us superfluous to what in fact is the present and the future of these questions in American culture."

Paul Ramsey persisted in his claim that Niebuhr is relevant to—indeed, is needed by—our day. "I can just imagine," Ramsey said, "Reinhold Niebuhr having the courage and verve to condemn utterly, with great strength and persuasiveness, the single factorial interpretation of evil in human history that many people today have. This was illustrated recently by Beverly Harrison, who took the floor at a plenary session of the Society of Christian Ethics and condemned the Catholic bishops' statement on economic justice. Why? Not because of the matter of the ordination of women to the priesthood, but because the statement did not pronounce egalitarianism to be the absolute ideal. A single factorial interpretation of history—whether it be feminism or something else—is precisely the very thing that Niebuhr so powerfully and persuasively condemned."

The conferees appeared to agree that Reinhold Niebuhr's work remains instructive for activists, theologians, and churches, and for moral discourse in American public life. But the way in which it might be instructive remained to be settled. As Glen Thurow of the University of Dallas noted, "Richard Fox says that we shouldn't try to nurse Niebuhr into a feeble old age. It would be better for us to let him die, and then maybe we would see a glorious resurrection. But what I'm puzzled about is where the resurrection comes in."

THE POSSIBILITY OF MORAL DISCOURSE

The conference was now ready to shift gears—from a discussion of Reinhold Niebuhr to a discussion of moral discourse in America. This second discussion centered on a paper by Michael J. Sandel, who teaches in the Department of Government at Harvard University. It was Sandel's responsibility to get the group thinking about political philosophy.

He wasted no time in doing just that. "However difficult it is to conceive of the way in which moral discourse might inform our political life," Sandel declared, "it is unavoidable that political discourse in practice presupposes some answers to moral and sometimes theological questions. If moral and theological positions are inescapable in political discourse, then that recasts the way we think about the relation of moral discourse to politics." It was clear from the outset that Sandel was not pitching for strict separation between politics and moral-religious discourse.

A Certain Liberalism against Moral Discourse

Sandel next described a version of liberalism that aggressively pushes separationism: "The version of liberalism with which I'm concerned in my paper is a version that may be different from the one Niebuhr held, insofar as he was a liberal. It's a version of liberalism that's common in moral, political, and legal philosophy these days. It's also prevalent in our actual public life, our political debate. It can be summed up as a matter of political philosophy in the claim that the right is prior to the good in two senses. First, this version of liberalism holds that certain individual rights are so fundamental that they override considerations of the general welfare or the common good. Second—and this is the more powerful and controversial claim —it holds that it's possible to identify those rights according to principles of justice which don't themselves presuppose or depend on any particular conception of the good." The most sophisticated statement of this version of liberalism is *A Theory of Justice* by John Rawls.

"I argue against this claim," Sandel continued, "on the grounds that this conception of justice and rights presupposes a conception of the person or the self which is implausible and which cannot make sense of certain aspects of moral and political life. It cannot make sense of our capacity for moral agency, for reflection on and deliberation about ends and political purposes. And it cannot make sense of certain aspects of political community and moral and political obligation. Insofar as this liberalism's self is considered given prior to ends, purposes, aims, and attachments, to that extent the neutral state—the one that does not presuppose a conception of the good — is appropriate. But, as I argue, that conception of the self is implausible, and insofar as it is, I argue that that conception of politics and justice is implausible."

Sandel then proceeded to argue against his argument: "There are really two possible objections to this critique of liberalism. One of them says, 'Yes, the ideal of the neutral state or the procedural republic does presuppose this conception of the self,' and then defends it. It notes that freedom was granted by the Enlightenment, and freedom means avoiding entanglement in relationships and communal obligations. The second criticism doesn't support that Enlightenment conception of the self, but it denies that liberalism requires it. It says that it is possible to argue for the priority of right over good without erasing any particular conception of the self. As against Kantian, Enlightenment liberalism, this approach argues for what might be called pragmatic or minimalist liberalism. This argument is offered by Rawls himself and by philosopher Richard Rorty. So minimalist liberals say the case for liberalism is political, not philosophical or metaphysical: it doesn't depend on controversial claims about the nature of the self. Since people disagree about conceptions of the good, minimalist liberals reason, we should try to seek principles of justice that do not presuppose the validity of any particular conception of the good. Given the diversity of modern life, we are more likely to agree on the terms of the neutral framework than we are to resolve the debates about the common good.

"Minimalist liberals argue for a political conception of justice rather than a moral or metaphysical one. But I think we can best see how minimalist liberalism's political conception of justice is inadequate by considering a few examples—witchcraft, abortion, and the Lincoln-Douglas debates."

"The connections are obvious, of course," Neuhaus observed drily.

Undeterred, Sandel continued. "What would the political argument be against burning witches? Remember that the political argument brackets the questions about whether there are such things as witches and, if so, whether it is for man or God to punish them. Whether burning alleged witches is just would depend on how best to secure the interest of social cooperation. Under most conditions this aim would most likely be served by banning the practice of burning at the stake, although it is conceivable that in some cases—perhaps including that of seventeenth-century Salem — witch-hunts could help rather than hurt the process of social cooperation.

"This example of witchcraft illustrates two problems with the idea of a political conception of justice. The first is that the case for toleration is left to depend on a political calculation about how best to secure social cooperation at any given time. But a second difficulty—and this has wider implications—is that the political conception seems to depend for its plausibility on an implicit answer to the question that it claims to bracket. At least the priority of this practical interest in social cooperation becomes far more reasonable if the bracketed question turns out a certain way. If there really were such things as witches, for example, it would be less reasonable to bracket theology and metaphysics in the first place. The more we are convinced that those who believe in witches are deluded, the greater our confidence in the case for bracketing the controversy about witches. The point here is that the political argument against witch-hunts secretly feeds on some degree of confidence in how those theological and metaphysical arguments come out.

"Consider now a case much closer to home—the case of abortion. Given the intense disagreement in our society over the moral permissibility of abortion, this would seem a case tailor-made for a political solution that brackets the moral and religious issues, that is neutral with respect to them. But with abortion as with witchcraft, the plausibility of the case for ascending or retreating to neutral ground hardly depends on which moral or religious conviction is true. If human life in the relevant moral sense really does begin at conception, then bracketing the moral-theological question of when human life begins or setting it aside for political purposes is far less reasonable than it would be if given rival moral and religious assumptions. The more confident we are that fetuses are, in the relevant moral sense, different from babies, the more confident we can be in affirming a political conception of justice that sets aside the controversy about the moral status of fetuses. The debate itself reflects this sense in which even a supposedly political conception of justice is parasitic on a certain view of how those controversies come out. The debate over abortion is not only about when human life begins but also over how reasonable it is to abstract from that question for political purposes. Opponents of abortion resist the translation from moral to political terms because they know that more of their view will be lost in the translation. The allegedly neutral territory offered by minimalist liberalism is likely to be less hospitable to their religious convictions than to those of their opponents. For defenders of abortion, however, little that is comparable is at stake. There is not that much difference between, on the one hand, believing that abortion is morally permissible, and, on the other, agreeing that as a political matter women should be free to decide the moral question themselves. The moral price of political agreement is much higher if one believes that abortion is wrong than if one believes that it is permissible.

"The last example—the argument by Stephen Douglas in the Lincoln-Douglas debate—may be the most famous of all cases that are arguments for bracketing such moral questions for the sake of political agreement. Douglas argued that since people are bound to disagree over the morality of slavery, national policy should be neutral. 'To throw the weight of federal power into the scale in favor of either the free or the slave states,' Douglas claimed, 'would violate the fundamental principles of the Constitution and run the risk of civil war.' The only hope of holding the country together, Douglas maintained, was to agree to disagree, to bracket the moral controversy over slavery. So Douglas was offering a case for the political conception of justice. Lincoln argued against precisely this idea of bracketing the moral question for political purposes. In the debates he contended that policy should express rather than avoid substantive moral judgment on slavery. Although Lincoln was not an abolitionist, he argued that government should treat slavery as the moral wrong it was and prohibit its extension to the territories. Douglas, on the other hand, claimed that, although from a personal moral viewpoint he was against slavery, for political purposes at least he was agnostic; he did not care if slavery was voted up or down. Lincoln replied that it was reasonable to bracket the question of the morality of slavery only on the assumption that slavery was not a moral evil.

"In the Lincoln-Douglas debates, as in the contemporary abortion debate, the moral question itself was not directly at issue. The Lincoln-Douglas debates were not about the morality of slavery; they were about whether to bracket a moral controversy for the sake of political agreement. Lincoln argued that the political conception of justice, which was defended by Douglas, depended for its plausibility on a particular answer to the substantive moral question it sought to bracket. Lincoln concluded his final debate with Douglas by posing this rhetorical flourish: 'Is it not a false statesmanship that undertakes to build up a system of policy on the basis of caring nothing about the very thing that everybody does care the most about?'

"That is an answer that can be made to those who defend minimalist liberalism: a political conception of justice, effective as it may be in the face of conflicting conceptions of the good, cannot avoid presupposing some answers to the moral and sometimes theological conceptions that it purports to bracket. If that is true, then it is impossible to make a general case for separating politics from moral-philosophical-theological questions. And if that is impossible, it suggests a reason for attending to the possibilities and prospects of moral discourse."

"Marvelous!" Richard Neuhaus responded. Then he called for other—and longer—responses.

Since Stanley Hauerwas had a bone to pick with liberalism, he also had a bone to pick with minimalist liberalism as represented by Richard Rorty. After reading a paragraph by Rorty, Hauerwas criticized him: "In the very claim to develop a political conception of justice is in fact an account of the kind of people we ought to be. We ought to be nontotalitarian people who cannot make up our minds, who are capable of enjoying and understanding everything and making a decision about nothing. Behind that is the kind of justification that was also given by the pluralist political theorists of the 1950s for why pluralism is such a good thing." Unfortunately, Hauerwas contended, Niebuhr had taken in too much of this pluralist political theory.

Sandel noted that Rorty's defense of minimalist liberalism would be quite simple—"It works."

Neuhaus was quick to respond: "I'm reminded of Hannah Arendt's *Totalitarianism,* in which she quotes Jefferson's idea of heaven, which is the Senate being in perpetual session, rational men being locked in debate over the end of man and what we ought to do about it in time. The interesting thing is that in response to Rorty, we might say, 'No, it doesn't work in terms of what we want to do, which is to discuss the end of man and what we ought to do about it in time.' In other words, we want to discuss the common good, so it doesn't work for that." And that of course raises the democracy question: people in a democracy should be able to discuss politically what they want to discuss.

Minimalist liberalism can lead not only to antidemocratic practice, as Neuhaus suggested, but also to a radical autonomy, as Paul Ramsey warned: "One of the prime books in circulation in medical ethics these days is by a man straight out of the 1960s, when autonomy gets popularly announced. He doesn't believe in slavery anymore, but he believes it is perfectly right for a person to enslave himself as an expression of autonomy. That also has to be and is a test as to whether you believe in autonomy. This has to do with an honored profession that does not know how to recognize an abomination. If you no longer recognize abominations in a society, then you do not have anything bracketing any profession—lawyers, politicians, or anybody else."

David Novak was worried that minimalist liberalism sunders — both in theory and practice — rights from duties. Novak said, "If a right is my individual claim upon society, then it stands to reason that in order for my right to be fulfilled, someone has to regard it as a duty to answer my right. It seems that that duty can arise from one of two sources. It can be a deontological duty—namely, it can be the command of a sovereign, or a supreme sovereign, God. Or it can be a teleological duty—in other words, the reason that I fulfill my duty to help you claim your right is that we both regard it as good. And we regard it as good qua common good, which means we are basically answerable to social duties even before we claim our rights. This gives me the only rational basis for choosing to do my duty as opposed to being forced to do it.

"A right is meaningless unless it is a claim that is capable of being fulfilled. And it is not fulfilled by another individual claiming his or her rights. It is fulfilled by another individual who has already been totally socialized and who acknowledges duty. Then as I have indicated, the question becomes, 'What is the source of duty?' "

John Cooper then inquired, "Does it help in our understanding of what we mean by human rights to contrast them with what we could possibly mean by animal rights? With specific reference to the case of abortion, what would it be like to live in a future where the category of fetal rights as neither human rights nor some other kind of rights was an accepted norm?"

"Fetal rights," Sandel answered, "is not the best way of arguing against abortion. A wide range of other considerations are probably more pressing morally. In fact, rights discourse in general misses a lot that is morally at stake in the issue of abortion."

Novak jumped into the exchange and responded to Cooper's question about animal rights and fetal rights: "When you talk about fetal rights or animal rights, you are using the term 'right' very loosely. How can a living thing that cannot possibly make a claim have rights in the original sense of the term? Obviously, that animal or entity has a right because somebody else regards it as a duty to be concerned with that animal's or that entity's good. That's where the language of rights really breaks down. Used in its original sense, the word 'rights' presupposes rational adults who are capable of verbalizing their claims. Yet we are uncomfortable with the fact that that original terminology does not include aspects of our communal life that we believe are deserving of protection. It is precisely there that we must have a notion of duty and good to back up the language of rights, because that language, taken by itself, is not strong enough to maintain protection for such things as fetuses and animals, which, among other things, religious tradition has protected.

"Again, in its original sense, a right makes sense only if somebody can make a claim for that right. In the Greek, 'right' referred precisely to an individual's coming to the court and making a claim upon the citizens of Athens."

Jerome King of the University of Massachusetts changed the subject by asserting "the supremacy of the political over the philosophical. This is derived in some sense from the fact that the political finally deals with crisis events. I'm thinking of Augustine's comment in his recounting of the trial of Jesus before Pontius Pilate. The argument is that Pilate, recognizing Jesus as an innocent man, nevertheless sacrifices him to the mob because he, as governor, is responsible for public order. I guess the conclusion is that expediency is the name of the game in politics. Politics always has to be prior to philosophical considerations because it inherently concerns crisis. I don't know whether that bears on your argument or not, Professor Sandel."

Sandel coolly replied, "If it were true, it would bear on my argument. But then we would have to know more about what is at stake when expediency is invoked. Expediency is a consideration that has to do with extreme means being required, presumably for the sake of important ends. What the ends actually are is typically assumed or taken as given when we invoke expediency or necessity, but they are always in the background."

After King stated that order is the assumed good, Sandel elaborated: "But there is order and there is order. There are all kinds of order—some more and some less worth preserving at the cost of extraordinary means. I'm not sure there's any such thing as plain order, which is undefended, unjustified, and unlegitimated." Again, Sandel's point was the inevitability of moral-philosophical concerns in matters political.

Selves and Republics

A new set of questions was put on the table by John Hittinger. "I am about to utter a heresy," he confessed. As the participants chuckled and braced themselves for a heretical utterance, he continued, "Even though I'm from Illinois, I have a problem with Lincoln's legacy. I'm not going to defend Douglas's position or say that slavery is good or should be bracketed. I happen to think the Civil War is the greatest event of our history. But in his paper Professor Sandel marked the development of the national republic from the time of the Civil War, and claimed that the failure of the national republic brought on the procedural republic. I'd like to suggest that Lincoln is partly responsible for this.

"Think of Robert E. Lee, who said that he favored neither slavery nor succession, and that he would not draw his sword against fellow Virginians. In Lee's statement there is a political theory that we should consider. I think I can say, without romanticizing the Old South, that the Civil War was a turning point where this theory subsided, where loyalties were broken down sociologically and economically. There are ideological parasites feeding on Lincoln's philosophy, which is a sound philosophy. Because of them, we have lost any kind of identity that is particular or regional. At best we can undertake rearguard actions to try to hang on to the traditions. Perhaps a certain view of the church as a form of community that can stand against rootlessness is a possibility. You see, liberalism is not a spent force. It assumes, like Rorty, that its philosophy will work if we can just shed the particularities that have been put on us."

Concentrating on conceptions of the self, Sandel responded to Hittinger: "You offered Robert E. Lee as an example of someone who has a particular identity that gives rise to moral and political obligations. This position has a poignancy that we can appreciate and even admire, quite apart from any sympathy —or lack thereof—that we might have for his actual choice. The tragic character of Lee's position seems to be an illustration of the way in which we, in order to make sense of tragic dilemmas of this kind, acknowledge that Lee had conflicting self-under-standings and obligations. If we took Lee's loyalty or identity as a Virginian as it weighed in this tragic balance and redescribed it as the object of a choice or an end which an antecedently iden-tifiable self claimed or affirmed, then we would drain the pos-sibility of tragic choices such as the ones Lee confronted from moral discourse. Why? Because there would be no self who would be claimed even as he deliberated, but only selves who had ties and obligations that flowed from choices.

"It would have been interesting if Lee had said, 'I will not raise my sword against another Christian,'" Stanley Hauerwas conjectured.

"Or 'I will not raise my sword against another American,'" Theodore Weber added. "After all, Lee was a graduate of the United States Military Academy."

Sandel followed with a query: "The question arises: What conception of justice and moral and political life is appropriate to situated selves, in contrast to the conception appropriate to selves conceived as freely choosing selves who are not claimed in advance by any particular identity? The neutral state is ap-propriate to unsituated selves but not to selves claimed or situated. To be sure, this raises a further question: What are the relevant communities that define us, and to what extent have we gone down a particular historical and cultural path so that now we have to strain to describe ourselves as defined in any meaningful way by claims and loyalties and obligations? This is a moral and cultural predicament insofar as we find ourselves incapable of understanding ourselves along such lines. It is something to worry about rather than welcome.

"In *The Human Condition* Hannah Arendt provides an answer to those who welcome the developments that lead to the unencumbered self. She speaks of behaviorism, and notes that the problem with behavior is not that it is false but that it might become true. That is the proper argument to be made against the unencumbered self. The point is not so much that it is false but that it is a characteristic drift in our political culture. The thing to worry about is that it might become true."

Then Professor Sandel backed up for a moment and retold a part of the American story. "The national republic," he began, "sought, in the hands of at least some of the Progressives, to enlarge the understanding of political community and to cast it on a national basis, whereas through the nineteenth century political community was largely developed through smaller forms of association. By the turn of the century it was clear that democracy and liberty, which had depended on decentralized arrangements of power, were threatened by the concentration of power in the corporate economy. Political unity was disempowered by developments in the scale of economic life. The answer to that predicament—which was completed more or less, in principle at least, in the New Deal, although extended in the time since — was to provide a rival concentration of power in the nation-state and in the federal government. The aspiration was to make political power a match for economic power."

It is possible that the national republic created as many problems as it solved, or so Sandel suggested: "Today there is a free-floating but unacknowledged disillusionment or frustration with this arrangement. Much of our debate is cast in the terms that the procedural republic offers — that is, rights-oriented terms. People disagree about what rights matter most. In this debate, conservatives put the emphasis on property rights and certain individual rights, whereas liberals put the emphasis on social, economic, educational, and welfare rights. In both camps the discourse of rights largely dominates, although there is a difference of opinion over which scheme of rights will best realize the ideal of the state as a neutral framework within which individuals can choose their own ends and purposes. But what this debate takes for granted is the concentration of power both in the economy and in government. Conservatives have been critical of the concentration of power in the welfare state; liberals have been critical of the concentration of power in the corporate economy. But each has had a blind eye where the other has had a critical eye."

If the national republic and its progeny, the procedural republic, are inadequate and unsatisfactory models of political life, where might correctives be sought? Sandel responded, "The answer is to try to arrive at ways—or at least to debate politically the question of how—to address the fact that we suffer from and are frustrated by a double disempowerment. It has to do with a concentration of power in both the corporate economy and the bureaucratic state. In order to reconstitute more meaningful forms of political participation, we need to scale back both of those forms of power. That's difficult to do because it requires forms of association with which people actually identify. And it raises a significant question: Are there meaningful forms of identity that are more than merely private, individualistic forms, and could they be linked to forms of political community and participation?

"What we have now is a great gap between the terms of our collective identity, which is more and more privatized and individualistic, and the actual scale on which our political and economic life is conducted, which is increasingly distant and comprehensive. We need to work on easing this gap from both directions: we need to go to the sources of tradition and identity that could sustain a way of life broader than the merely privatized while at the same time connecting that way of identifying ourselves with actual forms of political community that could sustain and cultivate and be hospitable to enlarged self-understanding. The problem is that each seems to await the other. Finding those forms of political community seems to depend on having those enlarged self-understandings, but cultivating those self-understandings seems to depend on having political arrangements that sustain them. So we have to figure out a way of working from both directions at once."

Still thinking about the case of Robert E. Lee, Ronald J. Sider of the Eastern Baptist Theological Seminary challenged the group to take on another case study. "Let's switch the particulars," said Sider, "and talk about Hitler's Germany and a German general who was opposed to Nazism. That raises a question: If you have no way of getting beyond competing situated selves, then you really cannot object to the German general making exactly the same decision that Lee did."

Neuhaus asked, "Against whom would the German general not raise his sword?"

Sider replied, "Against the German people. Just as Lee would not raise his sword against fellow Virginians, the German general would say, 'I hate Nazism, but I cannot kill Germans, so I'll join Hitler's army.' "

"In the case of the German general," Sandel said, "it is conceivable that we would have to hear his story. We would have to read his letters. There were some German generals, I imagine, who were torn because they saw their obligation to the German nation, understood in some historical way, as opposing Hitler."

Paul Ramsey inserted a point: "Dietrich Bonhoeffer's midnight talks about whether to join the plot against Hitler would be an example of what Professor Sandel is talking about."

Still puzzled, Sider asked if "there is a norm beyond different situated selves on the basis of which one might object. Should Lee have appealed to a higher norm and made a different decision?"

Sandel answered, "Lee would not have needed to appeal to a norm higher than his situation to make a different decision. To the contrary, what he saw as the competing obligation to his obligation to Virginia—the thing that gave him pause, that made him torn—was the fact that he was an officer in the Union army and believed in the United States of America and believed in the U.S. Constitution. What you're looking for, Ron, is a more universal appeal. Those appeals are understandable in the light of situations, though perhaps more general ones. An example is one's identity as a member of the human community or the human family, as defined by various religious traditions. But those are also situated conceptions."

Continuing the point, Roger Shinn sketched China's implicit value system. The Chinese are so entirely situated, he noted, that they don't even have a word for "privacy." They are unable to conceive of the individual apart from his or her various communities. This suggests, Shinn needled, "that there are more affinities between Chinese communism and neoconservatism than we often recognize."

Sandel did some needling of his own in response: "I'm shifting uncomfortably in my chair because I think of myself neither as a defender of the procedural republic and the unsituated self nor as a Chinese communist — nor, worse, as a neoconservative." This comment was followed by some good-natured laughter.

When the dust had cleared, Shinn offered a modest defense of proceduralism. His authority was none other than

Reinhold Niebuhr, who "stated his case for toleration in an article for *Christianity and Crisis*. Niebuhr wrote that if he had to pick from Christian history a best example of the relation of theology to politics, it would be the left-wing Puritans of seventeenth-century England. He gave two reasons. One was that Milton and others argued on theological grounds for the integrity of the person and for the importance of not forcing certain beliefs on people against their will. Then, in a characteristic Niebuhrian twist, he gave the second reason: What they did not accomplish, the providence of God accomplished for them, in that the sects were in themselves so diverse that one of them couldn't get away with imposing its beliefs on others. That, in a sense, is proceduralism given a theological interpretation."

"That's providential proceduralism," observed Neuhaus.

William Miller reminded the group that Niebuhr developed another case for toleration in *The Nature and Destiny of Man* in a section entitled "Having and Not Having the Truth." Miller elaborated: "Niebuhr thought you needed both to affirm a substantive truth and to welcome conflicting concepts of the good that restrict your imperialistic effort to realize your particular version of the good. He assumed that any conception of the good is going to be corrupt and tainted because it is possessed by a prideful self. Niebuhr believed that religious humility, though difficult to achieve, is the soundest ground of toleration. That's different from shoulder-shrugging toleration." According to Miller, Niebuhr admired Lincoln for his persistent humility, even in the Lincoln-Douglas debates and even on the issue of slavery.

Glen Thurow immediately disagreed with Miller's last point: "Lincoln's political project was to wipe off the face of the United States the opinion that slavery was good. He had no toleration for that opinion whatsoever. In fact, the result of his political effort is that nobody in the United States believes anymore that slavery is good. Lincoln succeeded in wiping that opinion out of our public-political existence. That was his aim, and it has nothing to do with tolerance. After all, Lincoln doesn't acknowledge that he might be wrong about slavery; he never says that. He's absolutely confident that he's right about slavery."

But sometimes, Paul Ramsey argued as he returned the group to twentieth-century concerns, what is called "toleration" is not very tolerant. "Look what happens to students who bring religious truths to a college campus," he challenged.

"They may hold these truths, but they get to be so private about what they believe. They have to respect the person right down the hall who has exactly the opposite opinion. So, the initial claim for truth gets buried in the socialization of college students." And it gets buried, one might add, under a heavy blanket of alleged toleration.

Neuhaus set forth yet another case for toleration: "Roger Williams is depicted in our civics textbooks as being a premature member of the ACLU—that's why he favored the separation of church and state. But it was precisely because he had the truth, because the saints had the truth, that church and state had to be separated, lest the unregenerate rule over the saints on matters having to do with the ultimate truth—namely, the way of salvation. In that sense, toleration in the form of the separation of church and state was most distinctly a religious achievement motored by a very intense and passionate commitment to a truth, which dare not be made subject to an inevitably corrupting influence of state power."

Ramsey was now ready for the conference to do away with nuance and qualification. So he asked a bottom-line question: "We are all opposed to the present situation in our republic, aren't we?" Without taking a head count of those who agreed, he issued something like a call to arms: "That being the case, at least we ought to try to get together with one another, to get over all the religious animosity of the past, and to do something in the public forum with the neutral state we have. Isn't that right? But I don't hear of anybody doing it, except those in this room."

"We're just starting, Paul. We're just getting underway," Neuhaus suggested.

"Then I want to know who in the public forum is speaking up for Grove City College," Ramsey retaliated.

"Some of us are. And you are," Neuhaus answered.

Dissatisfied, Ramsey continued his offensive: "But I don't see anybody reaching out to evangelicals, or thinking that there is something fundamentally wrong in the public square—apart from the rightness or wrongness of discrimination. Even Catholic hospitals are now in severe danger of being required to allow abortions on their premises. Where is *Christianity and Crisis*? Why isn't it calling our attention to the manifest and continued success of the empty public square? But apparently we are so opposed to evangelicals—we think they're so crude. We're willing to say abstractly, 'I believe you are wrong, but I'll defend to the death your right to say or do thus-and-so.' But we're not willing to defend Grove City College or a Catholic hospital. Who in the world is really reaching out to those evangelicals?"

"The Center on Religion and Society," said Neuhaus whimsically but with a touch of pride.

And Christopher Wolfe added: "At least some of us want to get out there and use federal dictation to tell all hospitals— Catholic and non-Catholic alike — that they cannot perform abortions."

With a devious grin Michael Sandel then asked Ramsey, "What do you say to that?"

Ramsey replied, "We are in the procedural republic. But I don't see why in the world we have to continue to rail against the little enclaves of moral communities that are out there." That was a solemn point on which to end a discussion of the procedural republic known as the United States.

Cultural Shifts and Solutions

Richard Neuhaus kicked off the final phase of Michael Sandel's portion of the conference by returning to the American story of political power countering economic power. That story, Neuhaus urged, is not the whole story: "What got lost in this process was another kind of power—if you will, cultural power. Cultural power deals with political and economic power. But it has increasingly been driven from the public arena by the political construct and is now undergoing a similar kind of insurgency to challenge the political and economic deal that was struck. Thus we witness in American life today what I have called the 'bourgeois insurgency.' In its hardest, harshest form it is the Religious New Right. It is an insurgency of democratically based, religiously grounded beliefs about selves, community, and the world that most people thought we could always take for granted.

"Is it possible that at this moment in American life, in terms of the development of constructs of power, there is an effort—a democratically and even 'populistically' driven effort—to create a countervailing cultural power over against political and economic constructs? If it would not offend too much, I would propose that what's going on in this room and what Professor

Sandel's work represents is a kind of rationalization—in the best sense of the word, an intellectual and philosophical and moral legitimation at a very sophisticated level—of this cultural insurgency." This insurgency, it might be said, involves a Pareto-like (Vilfredo Pareto) circulation of cultural institutions and elites through which the Protestant mainline becomes the oldline and is moved to the sideline. Furthermore, Neuhaus noted, the insurgency may even lead to the era that will follow the procedural republic of today.

Generally, Sandel seconded Neuhaus: "I agree with the main thrust of that thought. We do seem to see this political and economic field being objected to by a cultural insurgency which feels that the present legitimation is inadequate and thus poses another. But I think it would be too bad if the Religious New Right was seen as the only or the primary carrier of this cultural insurgency. True, the Religious New Right is partly an expression of the insurgency. But the Religious New Right's insurgency is also partly symptomatic of the hollowness of a public life emptied of larger meanings, which is a result of political and economic arrangements. The alternative that one would want to hope for and argue for and defend is a much broader insurgency which would try to restore to our public life shared meaning of a kind that would not leave a vacuum that would invite narrower and more intolerant versions of this cultural response. So, granted, a cultural insurgency is occurring, but it is potentially broader than the expression of it we've seen to date. We need a political agenda to articulate it and draw it out and give it a constructive force."

Richard Fox asked Sandel for a clarification: "When you say 'broader,' do you mean 'secular'?"

"Not necessarily," Sandel replied. "Filling in the meaning of which public life has been emptied certainly needn't be and couldn't be wholly secular. I don't think it need be wholly religious either. Religion and different religious traditions in this country have an important part to play in defining the public philosophy that could animate the sort of public life that we see as necessary and yet missing. What one would want to see is a revitalized political debate which at the same time would involve explicit moral discourse, which in turn would be informed by different religious perspectives."

"Your response," noted Neuhaus, "is almost precisely the

same as the stated, constituting purpose of The Rockford Institute Center on Religion and Society—to tease out of this cultural insurgency the development of a new public philosophy that is morally informed."

This lofty goal soon attracted substantive criticism. Fox was the first to take aim. He wondered if today's cultural insurgency is really offering an alternative. "In *The Naked Public Square*," he explained, "Richard Neuhaus shows that the evangelical Right is deeply imbued with therapeutic, consumerist sorts of ideals. It is very 'this-worldly.' Its preaching is about health and success, not transcendent judgment and that sort of thing. This is where Niebuhr is perennially relevant. He maintained that the churches are part of the problem; they're not just some simple solution. I take Neuhaus and Hauerwas to be saying that too. They're saying that we need churches that are much leaner and meaner—that is, churches of the catacombs, not some Constantinian sort of churches."

Hauerwas quickly joked that Fox had better watch how he associated people. Then the Duke professor claimed, "I'm leaner, but Neuhaus is meaner." The latter promised to "leave that alone" as the laughter became uproarious.

Roger Shinn was the second to criticize the public philosophy proposed by Sandel and Neuhaus. Although harboring some sympathy for the proposal, Shinn said that he sees "some very strong reasons, including moral reasons, why society has gone the direction of the procedural republic. That original moral consensus of the civic republic was not as good as it might appear to us in our more nostalgic moods. Obvious flaws come to mind: women weren't franchised, and slavery was authorized. Look at it this way. All of us yearn for a moral consensus if we're convinced that we're going to be part of it. If we're not going to be part of it, however, it looks oppressive to us. But we can't always mount an onslaught against it in the name of another moral consensus; we may not have a chance that way. So we may mount an onslaught in the name of the procedural republic."

Shinn then confessed that every January he argues with himself about whether or not he should renew his membership in the ACLU: "Behind this is the fact that in the 1960s I spent a considerable amount of time in court, at the request of ACLU lawyers, defending the rights of resisters to the war in Vietnam and the draft. In doing that, I always agreed with the side the ACLU lawyers took in the cases, and yet I felt uneasy that their legal philosophy was that of the unencumbered self. I don't want an unencumbered self. I don't want to be unencumbered myself. But I also don't want to have a bunch of encumbrances foisted on me by somebody else. That is a persuasive reason why we have gone this direction."

Neuhaus commented on Shinn's story, remarking that when Shinn was in court, it was almost as if he was playing a let's-pretend game, because to have standing he had to exclude religious encumbrances. Then Neuhaus recounted a recent game of judicial let's-pretend: "This past week a lawyer from Minnesota called me up. He told me that he'd just won a case, but his conscience was bothering him. The case had to do with a statue of justice that's been in one of the city parks for about a hundred years. At the base of the statue are the two Tablets of the Law—the Ten Commandments. Lo and behold, a woman backed by the ACLU brought a case against the city, claiming that the statue had to be taken down because it promoted the establishment of religion in a city park. The case went to court, and the city won. But it won—and this explains why the lawyer's conscience was bothering him—by making the argument that the Commandments were not significantly religious. The game was 'Let's pretend that nobody believes the Commandments anymore,' and the judge agreed to play let's pretend, knowing perfectly well that the argument wasn't true. So the judge ruled that the Commandments were not significantly religious and therefore that the statue did not violate the establishment-of-religion clause."

Shinn responded by finishing his critique of Sandel and Neuhaus. He said that infusing "a moral consensus is fine if it's not going to be imposed on unwilling people. At that point the result will often go in the procedural direction. I'm tempted to quote the old saying that politics is the art of finding proximate solutions to ultimately insoluble problems, which was uttered by somebody who's been mentioned occasionally today. Maybe your objectives shouldn't be too ambitious. Maybe you shouldn't try to make the state a secularized church."

Just before Sandel was to wrap up his portion of the conference, a little squabble erupted over Reinhold Niebuhr and the public order. Paul Ramsey, relying on the historical research of

Robert Handy of Union Theological Seminary, eased into the conflict. "Reinhold Niebuhr," he claimed, "was the last theologian in this country who did and could speak in the public forum unembarrassed by pluralism, while addressing moral and political issues in an unembarrassed way from a theological and biblical point of view."

What are you talking about? John Cuddihy might have asked. But he didn't. Instead he pointed out that he had written a book, "the first forty pages of which is called 'The Niebuhr-Herberg Treaty.' There I show that Niebuhr was one of the first to be totally embarrassed by pluralism. I recommend the book to you—it's called *No Offense—Civil Religion and Protestant Taste.* For example, Niebuhr calls off proselytization totally. He was the first great theologian to do that."

Neuhaus then asked Ramsey why it was that Arthur Schlesinger and Sidney Hook—two who could hardly be considered religious types—thought so much of Niebuhr, a theologian?

Ramsey answered, "How come they became so soft the minute he died? The political realism born out of the heights and depths of Niebuhr's theology certainly infused Hans Morgenthau and others. Certainly they weren't convinced to become Christians, but Niebuhr wasn't concerned with that. But they were impressed with Niebuhr's message for the public order—and I'd like to know who could have that kind of influence today."

Speaking especially to Ramsey and Cuddihy, Neuhaus played mediator: "Let's stipulate, as the lawyers say, that we've got a very substantive disagreement"—about whether Reinhold Niebuhr was the last theologian to speak in the pluralistic public arena without embarrassment—"that we're probably not going to be able to resolve. But it's a very interesting one."

Setting aside the stipulation, Roger Shinn recalled that after Niebuhr's prime, Martin Luther King was able to speak morally and biblically in public without embarrassment.

In his concluding remarks, Michael Sandel returned to the idea of the self—this time to the too-encumbered self. "That term," he explained, "has to do with people who are so embedded in a parochial setting that they're altogether incapable of reflecting on alternatives or even being aware of the sense in which theirs is a local setting. People at that extreme are as unhelpful to public life as the wholly unencumbered self is on the other."

Then Sandel found the golden mean: "It would be best to

find an understanding that lies between the purely parochial, radically unreflective, situated self and the radically unencumbered self. Perhaps this intermediate self-understanding could best be described as the understanding of the reflectively situated self who realizes even as he reflects on two diverging paths in moral or political life that he is claimed by particular traditions, identities, and obligations. We are not merely creatures of particular situations that we inhabit insofar as we are self-conscious of our particularity as we reflect. We appreciate the distinctiveness of the identity out of which we act and reflect. And by virtue of this reflectiveness or self-consciousness we are alive to other ways and wider horizons.

"Reflectively situated selves would not resist embarrassment in the face of pluralism. From their standpoint, to be embarrassed by pluralism seems morally admirable and politically desirable. I'm not talking about being embarrassed out of my convictions, but at least being embarrassed insofar as I am self-conscious enough to be reflective and alive to other ways of life and conviction that surround me."

Sandel then recalled Shinn's worry that a moral consensus which would include everyone would have to be imposed. "That's a worry that's important to bear in mind. Rather than aiming at a moral consensus, the cultural revolution that Richard Neuhaus speaks of should aim at a moral argument or a political argument informed by moral perspectives. That seems to me different from a moral consensus, because the expectation is not agreement but the quality and the character of the discourse, which is transformed insofar as it is explicitly informed by religious and moral traditions."

Someone asked, "Do you really want to say that the expectation is that there will be no agreement?"

"Certain things have to be shared in order to reach even disagreements," Sandel responded. "For example, people have to share a common language in order to disagree."

This reference to a common language set off Stanley Hauerwas: "Earlier we used the term 'the common good.' The definition always conjured by 'the common good' is broad, shared values and principles. I think that's a fundamental mistake in terms of the classical account, which involves much more of a sense of being able to articulate a common history. That is, a people share a story that gives them a way of talking about the diversity of the community necessary for it to find a way into the future. Therefore, the common good, according to the classical account, does not require that children be wanted and that abortion be considered against this good. Rather, it indicates that there is a people who feel that they have some goods to pass on to their children, which is in fact a history."

But then Christopher Wolfe wondered if having a story is enough. "Is that the ultimate criterion? Don't you have to evaluate the story? Don't you have to have some kind of substantive agreements?" he asked.

Sandel wanted to get back to discussing reasons for not aiming at a moral consensus, and he got his way because he was the presenter. He knew of two arguments against aiming at such a consensus: "First, the only way of achieving that in our society would be by imposition. Second, any moral consensus that would be achievable would be so thin that it wouldn't do justice to the richness and the depth of the convictions that one would want to animate moral discourse in public life. So that is why the goal is a shared language, or history, or narrative, something that is not merely descriptive or morally empty but rather infused with competing interpretations about the good we aim at. That is a more suggestive way of describing the purpose of such an enterprise, which is more productive than seeking a moral consensus or an agreement on minimal principles."

"But there's always an element of imposition, isn't there?" asked Neuhaus with a note of Niebuhrian realism.

"Yes, in the sense that certain laws and policies ultimately result, but everything depends on what justifies them," responded Sandel.

Hauerwas joined the conversation again: "So the textbook issues are at the heart of the matter. They raise the question about whether we can have a viable public education. If you have to say No to that question, I'm not sure that you have a viable republic at all."

As Neuhaus noted, the second quarter of the conference ended "on a Gibbonesque note of decline and fall."

A CATHOLIC CONTROL: JACQUES MARITAIN

Day two of the conference got underway with an introduction by Richard Neuhaus. "In the testing of things," he explained, "you always have to have a control group, or a control factor. So we thought that in our discussion of Niebuhr we'd need a papist control factor. We might have taken John Courtney Murray as a control, but we figured that Murray is enough of a presence here. After all, we have his chief campaign manager in George Weigel here, so Murray will no doubt sneak in without separate billing. Jacques Maritain is the one who has separate billing." And Maritain's case would be made by Ralph McInerny.

McInerny began by comparing Maritain's stature to Niebuhr's. McInerny's point was that in the twentieth-century American Roman Catholic community, Maritain functioned as a "role model" of sorts, much like Niebuhr functioned in the mainline Protestant community. Furthermore, McInerny continued, "Maritain became a Roman Catholic under the influence of a French writer who is largely unknown now, Léon Bloy. Bloy wrote a novel called *The Woman Who Was Poor,* which we all read in those days. It ended with a famous line: 'There is but one tragedy—not to be a saint.' When Maritain lectured, taught, and visited, that motto seemed to be brooding over his life. He was for many of us a symbolic figure and a role model, I guess we would say now."

McInerny went on to describe Maritain's vocation: "Thomism is a very comprehensive and universal approach— the approach Maritain took as a philosopher. We can speak of him as a philosopher of history; his aesthetic works are well-known. He was a metaphysician, a moralist, a political philosopher. He defined a philosopher in the grand sense—as one who reflects on and is involved in culture." One of Maritain's lifelong concerns, said McInerny, was the rights of man. McInerny elaborated: "For Maritain the rights of man are, in effect, the secularization of religious ideals. That's a simplification and a generalization, but I think it's true nevertheless. Usually 'secularization' is a term we use to deplore a development. So in order to show that Maritain didn't see the secularization of religious ideals as something to lament, we could call it the desacralization of certain truths which have been learned from the gospel but which are not tenable solely on the basis of Christian faith. Accordingly, for Maritain democracy is—in one of his more catchy phrases—the best political expression of the gospel. That remark excited a great deal of opposition among Roman Catholics because of the tendency to oppose the notion that a particular political expression is entailed by religious belief. Although Maritain didn't use the word 'entail,' he no doubt thought of democratic political development in the West as progressive in its incorporation of gospel ideals minus the gospel. He didn't think that was bad. On the contrary, he saw it as a real advance, because it enables people who are of different religious persuasions and/or those who have none to enter into practical and political agreement."

Rights and Law, Naturally

McInerny continued his point: "Maritain believed that it's possible to have an agreement on certain rights which does not entail a single sort of rational justification of those rights, or a single view of the person which would be the basis for asserting that human beings have those rights. So, on the first level he would say that he's waiving the question of meaning and assuming that all people mean the same thing by those rights and the phrases describing them. They could still be in deep disagreement about what they thought was the basis or ground for having those rights. In other words, one individual might have an atheistic approach to the person, another a theistic approach, another a Christian approach, yet another an Islamic approach, and so forth. These would all be quite different justifications for having these rights, but that wouldn't matter. We could still have a practical agreement."

McInerny went on to point out that, although Maritain was tolerant of all justifications of natural rights, he believed that only one actual justification exists—the natural-law tradition. "So he was one of the Thomists of recent times who have tried to put together the natural-rights tradition and the natural-law tradition. That's a very difficult thing to do, because the rights tradition deals with the unsituated person, whereas the natural-law approach obviously deals with the situated person. According to natural law, persons aren't just isolated and anonymous units that come over the horizon, meet, and enter into social contract; it's not as if we don't know where they came from. In the natural-law tradition there's the obvious realization that human beings are the result of the mating of adults of different genders and are born into families. That's what being an individual means. If progeny weren't nurtured by older people, they wouldn't survive to the point of being able to read the social contract. Given its emphasis, the natural-law tradition can't help but see the natural-rights tradition as somewhat unrealistic. The latter treats human beings as isolated, unsituated individuals, and then tries to put them together in terms of a contract."

Furthermore, McInerny added, "What Maritain wants to argue is this: not only is the natural law the only true theoretical grounding for talk of human rights, but also everybody, deep down inside, is an adherent of natural law. The possibility of political agreement exists because there is a structural, ontological, genuine similarity among people. Thus, as Maritain sees it, natural law is the basis for pluralism. In discussing natural law, what you do is show an individual that he's already committed to it, at least in the main, and that his practical discourse honors it implicitly. It's not a matter of persuading anybody to accept natural law, because that would presuppose that a principle exists prior to it by virtue of which you would say that natural law is a nice thing to have. Thus, real honest-to-God agreement among human beings is possible because human beings are human beings."

Neuhaus then offered an illustration of Maritain's point as McInerny had explained it. "Recently," Neuhaus reported, "the Center cosponsored with the Woodrow Wilson Center a conference at the Smithsonian. During that conference there was a very interesting exchange between Peter Berger of Boston University and David Little of the University of Virginia. The question of natural law was very much a part of the discussion of moral purpose and foreign policy. Berger, who by his own admission is no philosopher, was very skeptical about all of this natural-law business. 'What does it really do for you?' was his principal question. 'I've talked with these Thomists,' he said, 'and they come up with their just-war criteria based on natural law. But most of it is just common sense. If I take a certain situation—what ought to be done in South Africa, for example—my common sense tells me that such and such will work or won't work, or that such and such is appropriate or inappropriate.' David Little, very insightfully, said something like this: 'But Peter, you've just vindicated natural law. The point is precisely that it is commonsensical, and that it squares with your perception of how the world is, and what's possible and appropriate in terms of action in the world.' "

McInerny completed his introductory remarks by explaining how Maritain related natural law and Christianity. "The relationship between natural law and Christianity involves a kind of distillation of certain truths that most of us learn in our religious traditions but that we have come to see as incumbent and that people recognize as independent, in principle at least, of religious tradition. Since, for Thomas Aquinas, the Tablets of the Law are precepts of natural law, the question arises, Why were they revealed? The great paradox of the natural-law tradition is this: It was necessary—necessary for practical reasons— that the natural law be revealed and achieve divine sanction even though the argument is, in principle, that it doesn't require such sanction. Paradoxical as that might sound, that corresponds to our own experience. After all, if we try to imagine certain very important issues of our time being settled independently of the support of the religious tradition—like civil rights and abortion and sexual morality — if we try to imagine relying solely on natural reason or on our ability to figure out what our moral destiny is apart from our religious traditions, then I think we can appreciate the paradox of natural law. It seems almost to require the religious setting, although it isn't intrinsically dependent on it."

Paul Ramsey then talked about how Maritain's natural law "depends upon a sense of justice and a sense of injustice. Niebuhr also assumed this sense of justice and injustice. According to Maritain, the human mind knows natural law by inclination or disinclination. For example, when General Patton—and I hope he did this—marched the German burghers through a concentration camp, that old son of a bitch presumed those German hearts were touched by the injustice of it, no matter how acculturated to the contrary they had been."

Christopher Wolfe noted that one long-standing criticism of natural law is that the concept is too rationalistic. But, said Wolfe, Ramsey's comment on inclination erred in the opposite direction by investing too much hope in a natural sense of justice. Wolfe continued, "Saint Thomas notes that even one of the broad principles of natural law—Do not steal—could be completely obscured in an entire culture by custom. The classic example he used was Caesar's comment about the Germans and theft. Caesar claimed that stealing was a way of life among the Germans. But if all humans have a natural sense of justice, how could this be? Well, that sense is important, but it's more than just a gut feeling universally distributed among human beings. After all, culture shapes our feelings to such a significant extent that the mind must play a role, must reflect on such inclinations to correct distortions that often exist. You can't ignore the rational element."

Stanley Hauerwas objected to Wolfe's division of feeling and thought. "Aquinas believed that the mind desires," Hauerwas noted; "inclination is a rational business. For Aquinas the passions are rational. They're a part of the mind."

McInerny agreed and commented, "The mind is a nature first of all—before it is a mind, so to speak. There are certain immediate moves that it makes willy-nilly."

Then McInerny referred again to Aquinas, who "distinguishes two kinds of wisdom and gives an example from the practical order. If you have a problem regarding chastity, he argues, there are two things you might do. You might speak to a chaste man, or you might speak to a moral theologian—and they might even be the same person."

"A somewhat improbable possibility, perhaps," Neuhaus observed.

Surviving the moderator's one-liner, McInerny concluded, "Thomas is saying that there are two ways of addressing the question. Presumably, the chaste man would think about it and say, 'You know, what I would do is . . .' That's judgment through inclination. On the other hand, a moral theologian would appeal to a principle and give a kind of argument. The great danger is this: If you say that natural law is apprehended by knowledge through inclination, then you can get into the position of saying that only the good apprehend it. In a sense, of course, that's true. Some principles of natural law presuppose a subjective condition. But there are also some principles of natural law that are inescapable."

Earlier Ramsey had alluded to Niebuhr's view of natural law. Now Charles Brown probed that issue. "Niebuhr wasn't completely oblivious to natural law, although he didn't emphasize it. He did speak of a limited natural law, or freedom and equality as regulative principles of justice. In fact, he criticized—or ridiculed—Karl Barth for saying that we could get the moral law contained in the Ten Commandments only through the Bible; Niebuhr pointed out that Cicero could apprehend those norms. The problem that Niebuhr had with natural law could be traced to Saint Paul's comment on the war between the law in my members and the law in my mind." Brown even spotted an assumption of natural law in the first half of one of Niebuhr's famous sentences—"Man's capacity for justice makes democracy possible, and man's inclination to injustice makes democracy necessary." If Niebuhr assumes a natural law, said John Hittinger, it's an awfully thin natural law that he assumes. Why is that? Because, answered Hittinger, "Niebuhr doesn't relish enough particular goods. I'm bothered by the terms 'pretensions to virtue,' 'self-interest,' and so on. What I like about Maritain is that he can look at a particular good—at the good of a particular community or a particular interest—and say that that is proper, that that is good. For example, it is good that you love your wife; it is good that you love your state. I think again of Robert E. Lee —it is good and right that he love the state of Virginia. That isn't a Niebuhrian pretension to virtue, nor is it naked self-interest. It's part of the divine and natural order."

At that point Jerome King indicated why Niebuhr had a theory of the good that's too thin for most natural lawyers: "He was convinced, like Augustine, that language itself is an instrument of power and can never be anything but an instrument of power." And as an instrument of power, language is always capable of abusing and of being abused.

Next Sidney Callahan recounted an incident: "Recently I was in a debate with Beverly Harrison on the question of abortion. Before I even had a chance to talk, she totally dismissed me by saying, 'Well, of course Sidney Callahan is a natural-law theorist.' I immediately stood up and protested that that could never be said of me because I didn't know anything about it. Now I can see that I was like Peter—the apostle, not Berger— when he denied Christ." After a few seconds, or minutes, the laughter had died down enough so that Callahan could finish her point: "Now I can see that I am a natural-law theorist because of total conviction. Things that I'm reading in psychology now are moving away from relativism and toward the sense that there is a human nature and that certain emotions are programmed into us all, in all places at all times. New studies in cognition show that affection and cognition get fused very early. All this is resonating with what I'm hearing about Maritain." Natural law, as Maritain surely would have expected, seems to be breaking out all over the place.

On Power and America

Stanley Hauerwas now took it upon himself to cross-examine Ralph McInerny. "Tell us a little about Maritain's reflections on power," Hauerwas urged. "Niebuhr, as you know, was always thinking about inherent imbalances of power."

McInerny answered, "When Maritain thinks of power, he's thinking of the structure of moral decision and responsibility—that is, of being answerable for what we do. One ought to have the power to make one's own moral decisions—that is, one ought not be interfered with. Maritain's theory of democracy goes like this: The more people can participate in the choices and decisions that make up the onward flow of human life, the more people are able to function more fully as people, as moral agents. In other words, Maritain thinks of power in terms of the capacity for moral agency rather than in terms of social trade-offs."

"Do you see that as a weakness?" Hauerwas asked.

"No," replied McInerny. "The question is how to square that with Niebuhr's picture of power, which is the dominant picture. I've often thought that the civil rights movement, which began with a very overt appeal to our sense of the dignity of the human person, seems to have gotten into a kind of power-politics model, with trade-offs and all."

Hauerwas suggested that Niebuhr was so absorbed by the politics among nations that his idea of power was determined by such. On the other hand, Hauerwas proposed, "Maritain avoided reflections on international relations because he didn't have the conceptual tools to deal with them." Is that statement fair or unfair? Hauerwas wondered.

McInerny, the diplomat, responded: "It's both fair *and* unfair. Certainly Maritain did a lot of practical work on international statements. Actually he strongly favored the idea of world government."

"The prosecution rests!" William Miller announced to some boisterous laughter.

Theodore Weber got the group settled down with an observation: "Maritain didn't deal successfully with the problem of how power moves from the level of the nation-state to that of world public authority. He could see the logic, but he wasn't eager to tell us how that was going to happen." Niebuhr's problem was different from Maritain's, said Weber, since Niebuhr argued on theological and pragmatic grounds that nations shouldn't go to a world public authority.

George Weigel offered another comment on Niebuhr and world government: "It's very instructive to read the reflections of both Niebuhr and Maritain on their experiences at UNESCO from 1946 to 1948. Niebuhr speaks of the necessity of a vision of the political community transcending national boundaries and the impossibility of its final achievement. Unfortunately, there's a tendency to reduce Niebuhr to a realism blown up to 10,000 meters; this has to be resisted here. After all, in 1944 Niebuhr wrote that 'a purely realistic approach to the problem of world community offers as little hope of escape from anarchy as a purely idealistic one.' It's not quite as neat as these 'the-prosecution-rests' statements might lead us to believe."

Yes, agreed William Miller, "Niebuhr isn't into social physics. He isn't a kind of Machiavelli. And he isn't just into international relations. Look back at his ethics of the privileged class in *Moral Man and Immoral Society*; that ought to be brought out and read again today."

Roger Shinn then pointed to the depth and the source of Maritain's realism: "Maritain did take his Thomism seriously. He began one of his books by saying, 'I'm not a neo-Thomist; I would rather be called a paleo-Thomist; through this I am a Thomist.' No Thomist is innocent of the realities of power. Saint Thomas was not a perfectionist, not a utopian. He assumed that the business of government is to deal with a world of sinners, and that one function of government is to require people to do what they don't want to do; in fulfilling such requirements, people may learn to like what they ought to do. That's a beautiful premodern statement of what sociologists often say: behavioral change precedes attitudinal change. In his treatise on law Saint Thomas assumes that he's dealing with a world of sinners. Consider his doctrine of private property. In an unfallen world we wouldn't need any property. But because this is an imperfect world, we've got to have property, and that presumes instruments of power. Also, the doctrine of just war, like it or not, certainly assumes a role for power."

John Hittinger also let it be known that he had reason to oppose the stereotypes of Niebuhr the hard realist versus Maritain the soft idealist. "The first books by Maritain and

Niebuhr—*Integral Humanism* and *Moral Man and Immoral Society*
—came out in the 1930s," Hittinger noted. "Both men were very
impressed with the Marxist view that the proletariat is the class
that will be the just class. They thought it would make a new
society possible. They were both deeply impressed by the
economic and political crisis of the 1930s. In their books they explicitly stated that the proletariat—the working class—would
be the class to bring about justice. Eventually, however, they
both backed off from that position."

Still, for Richard Fox, Maritain was a little too idealistic
and a little too Pollyannaish. The issue was America, and Fox
had this to say: "I have trouble seeing the astuteness of
Maritain's observations on America. It strikes me that his observations may be very unastute. His observation that America
is not a materialist nation, for example, that we have all of this
spiritual potency, that we're always looking for something
more as a sign that we're not mere materialists—this seems
very implausible to me."

Then Fox offered his own observations on America: "As I
see it, one of the main perils—if not the main peril—that faces
us is precisely the ideology of growth, the ideology of spiritual
as well as material growth. We're compelled by the notion that
we're always supposed to be in the vanguard of lifestyle
changes, of spiritual changes, and that we're always supposed
to become something that we're not. This is built into our
economy and into our cultural attitudes." In Fox's opinion,
Maritain missed all of that—but Niebuhr didn't. "In the 1950s,"
said Fox, "Niebuhr was one of the key thinkers who maintained
tension in his view about America—unlike people like Daniel
Boorstin, who began celebrating the great American barbecue.
Maritain fit right into that 1950s celebration of America as the
greatest place on earth. Niebuhr resisted that."

McInerny replied, "I would feel that I misrepresented
Maritain if I described him as a cheerleader for America. But I
don't think it would be very astute for Maritain to say that this
is a materialistic country—that would be trivial. What I see as
astute is that he penetrated the clichés about America." Furthermore, McInerny noted, when Maritain gave the American experiment such high marks, he had in mind great American
writers and people such as Thomas Merton and Dorothy Day,
an extraordinary laity that hungers for contemplation.

Fox came back quickly: "Melville was fantastic, but nobody read him at the time. It was only later that he, like Thomas Merton, became a celebrity. To say that Merton is an example of spiritual revival is one side of the story. The other side is that he became a celebrity in a consumer culture. And spiritual consumption is part of the problem."

"If nobody read Merton, would that indicate that the society was more spiritual?" Neuhaus asked Fox.

Fox didn't answer Neuhaus, but he did respond to McInerny: "Dorothy Day is a better example. She's someone who's difficult for Americans to accept. Thomas Merton is easy to accept—he doesn't cost you anything. It does cost you something if you're going to follow Dorothy Day's example."

"It depends on what you mean by 'cost,'" McInerny protested. And besides, he said, Maritain saw the ambiguities, the dark side of American culture.

John Cuddihy sided with McInerny and opposed Fox: "Maritain would go right into the citadel of what you're talking about — the GNP, progress, and so on. He would say that American culture isn't materialistic, despite appearances. He was, after all, a Frenchman, and as such he knew what materialism is. And that's involvement—dense involvement—with money. People who have been to France and Paris know this. America isn't materialistic in that way. Maritain found an enormous, crazy, idealistic materialism in America. But it's a dematerialized materialism, and Maritain sensed that."

Richard Hutcheson, Senior Fellow of The Center on Religion and Society, stated that Maritain's emphasis on the common good is useful to those concerned with religion in a democratic public square. Maritain's work also goes a long way toward legitimating democracy. "But a defense of democracy," Hutcheson concluded, "has to contain an element of prophetic judgment, which was so much a part of Niebuhr's work." Hutcheson's point was clear: let Maritain complement Niebuhr and Niebuhr complement Maritain.

The Church's Public Speech

Christopher Wolfe of Marquette asked, "Should Catholic thought embrace rights vocabulary or rights rhetoric? Is that wise? Unquestionably, when the pope uses the term 'rights'

there's a big difference between what he means and what John
Locke meant. Certainly you want to talk to people in a
vocabulary that's available to them. But if you use that vocabulary, you're constantly having your meaning misunderstood
and coopted into a system of serious problems. Don't we need
to talk more about duties and be more careful about rights terminology precisely because rights talk is so easy for modern
people—for Americans—to use?"

Ralph McInerny replied that not only do popes use rights
talk but Vatican II does as well. "Therefore, it's not a matter of
our deciding *whether* we're going to use such talk; the point is
how we're going to use it." And the Catholic use of the public
vocabulary of rights, McInerny added, should include obligations and make clear to all concerned that it is not Lockean in
orientation.

It might be acceptable to use rights rhetoric, but no one
should take that as a sign of the church's sellout to a culture
fevered with all kinds of rights, contended William Lazareth.
"The Lutheran confessions insist upon the capacity of redeemed
human beings to join together with all persons of goodwill, who
are also created in God's holy and loving image, and to be as
realistic about grace as about sin. That puts us into a ballpark in
which we can insist, 'You cannot dehumanize me by rejecting
my understanding of humanity. I pay taxes too! And I want to
tell you about who I think we are together.' I suggest we not roll
over and play dead prematurely because other people are
rewriting the rules of the game in the public square."

"Luther's famous statement was that he would rather be
ruled by a wise Turk than by a foolish Christian," Neuhaus
repeated for the non-Lutherans in the group.

"That's the point," Lazareth the Lutheran agreed. "The
church's contribution to public life is to enlighten self-interest.
We're not going to replace self-interest. But we can offer some
insights into what constitutes enlightening, without absolutiz-
ing it into the bastardized anthropology of the Enlightenment,
which is godless."

Neuhaus then assumed the role of cross-examiner: "Are
you, Bill Lazareth, saying that you and all of us from our several
perspectives ought to go public with an understanding of
humanity and God's purposes? And what would that mean in
our kind of culture?"

Lazareth responded with conviction: "It means that I don't accept society's privatization of my piety as a personal hobby. We're now being reduced to a pietism as the only means for opposing secularism. But pietists and secularists are of the same genre. Both insist that religion is simply for the inner life and, if there is such a thing, for the afterlife. But both forget that this is God's creation and that we're not simply reductionists with regard to privatized redemption."

George Weigel, who had earlier been accused of being the resident campaign manager for John Courtney Murray, lived up to the billing: "I would take Lazareth's claim even further. It's not simply a matter of going beyond the privatized but of bringing our situatedness into public-policy discourse. That has to be done in a way that can be heard—if not by the Beverly Harrisons of the world then by people a little more willing than she may be to have a moral argument. That brings us back to the appeal of natural law. That offers a mediating language which may cut across what John Courtney Murray would have called the many conspiracies of American life. That would allow for agreement or disagreement rather than cacophony."

Agreeing with Weigel, Neuhaus turned to Lazareth and asked, "Bill, don't you need a mediating language? Do you want to argue in court about the nature of the unity of the Blessed Trinity? What about all of the people who say that they don't buy those presuppositions?"

Lazareth answered, "I'm saying that there's an area of overlap between all persons created in the image of God and some persons redeemed by God in Christ. That area of overlap should be the arena in which we engage in this power negotiation. In that negotiation I shouldn't have my biblical-theological-metaphysical presuppositions declared inherently illegitimate as an a priori."

"Nor should your public arguments be declared tainted because they're shaped by presuppositions that aren't shared by others," Neuhaus added as a friendly amendment. Lazareth accepted his point.

Glen Thurow went back to Wolfe's ground-breaking question and responded: "How far you adapt your language to the society around you depends in the first instance on how deep you think the problem goes. That is, if you look at the anti-abortion movement, if you look at the immediate problem—that is, saving all of those lives that are being lost—then you can see why there's a very great temptation to put the issue in right-to-life language. After all, it's readily understandable. People can grasp that that's important. And it's not very difficult to see that a fetus is a human life in some way. So these terms make a strong rhetorical argument. If, on the other hand, the problem involved in the issue of abortion goes deeper, if the abortion issue is not just a glitch showing that society has gone wrong in this particular area, if the abortion debate indicates that something more fundamental is at issue, then the rhetorical strategy becomes much more suspect. You can't reach the issues of the family, community, and communal justice with the language of right to life. In part the choice of rhetorical strategy depends upon how deep you think the evil goes.

"The other thing that has to be recognized is that when you speak in public, you always have to take into account that authority is present. In the United States that means a public authority of some sort. In the old days when you addressed a king you had to be careful about how you spoke, and I think that's still true in our democratic age. So how you proceed partly depends on how you understand public authority in the United States. That is, if you regard the current mode of the discussion of rights as the fundamental way of public discussion in the United States, then you're going to have a hard time getting away from it. Michael Sandel was suggesting that this was in fact only one part of our tradition. What he called civic republicanism was another part which would provide the way to get into some of these questions without speaking from outside the American political tradition. Within that tradition you can in a certain sense present your religious beliefs and convictions openly. Since participating in rule means joining the public discussion, civic republicanism seems to be open to all kinds of different views."

Thurow's statement triggered a response from Neuhaus: "If the situation is dire enough—for example, if the abortion debate is not a glitch or an inconsistency but rather is symptomatic of something that has gone radically wrong in public discourse, deliberation, and decision-making—then isn't it the case that Thomists, Lutherans, and others ought to enter the public square like gangbusters and say exactly what they think about the world and how it ought to work, and outline the appropriate moral conclusions to draw from that definition of reality? And isn't it the case that they shouldn't be too deferential in trying to translate or mediate their arguments into the language of those who would constrict the kind of arguments permitted in the public square? So they would say to the people, 'You have an obligation to understand my Thomistic argument just like I have an obligation to understand your argument. The point of our meeting as citizens is that we're going to respect one another's arguments, and part of that is trying to understand one another's arguments. But the thing you cannot do—and it isn't simply because I pay my taxes but because I participate constitutionally in this enterprise—is say that my way of argument, which has very venerable precedent and is not eccentric or idiosyncratic, is inadmissible in our debate.' "

On the business of when and how to make public language explicitly religious, Ralph McInerny urged discernment. "Sometimes it's unwise to bring forward explicitly religious conviction," he pointed out. "At other times it's required. There's no blanket rule that covers always and everywhere."

Sidney Callahan took McInerny's point in the direction of natural law: "When I debate with people on various issues, it may not be the best move to come out of the natural-law closet and say, 'Yes, I'm a natural-law *theorist*.' It might be better to use rights talk that is democratic, to talk like Saint Paul (who to the Athenians was an Athenian), to enrich this language, to fly the banner of common sense and experience. In other words, it might be best to be a natural-law *person*."

Then McInerny proceeded to lay down a blanket rule that covered another issue: "We should never drop the prophetic voice altogether. If we do, we're suggesting that religion is a marginalized, relatively unimportant aspect of our lives. Well, we don't think that because it isn't true. The basic thing is that we think Christianity is true, not just for us but for everybody. That's the evangelical, missionary side of the faith." And that's the side of the faith that's called into play when the church speaks in public about public concerns and crises.

NIEBUHR FOR TODAY

The last session of the conference was based on papers by Robin Lovin of Chicago and Stanley Hauerwas of Duke. It was during this session that the issue of Niebuhr's contemporary "relevance," to employ that overused word from the 1960s, was most decisively engaged. But first came some preliminaries. Lovin began by stating that the historical importance of Reinhold Niebuhr is not in dispute. "What is in dispute," he continued, "is the question of whether Reinhold Niebuhr offers important guidance for the contemporary task of religious social ethics. The question is whether he offers us ways of thinking about Christianity and society that can be separated from the particular opinions that he held about problems in his own time and that have some capacity for generalization beyond the social situation in which he wrote."

To those who say that Reinhold Niebuhr is compatible with all arguments and positions, Lovin said, "this conference is putting your image of Niebuhr to rest. I think of Waldo Frank's comment that when he tried to sort out Niebuhr in relation to his typologies of agapism, Niebuhr occupied all of the available positions. Frank concluded by noting that he would leave it to others to decide whether this multifacetedness spells richness or confusion of mind. This illustrates an important point about Niebuhr: No matter what we're doing, we can find a Niebuhr text to go with it. But what begins to emerge in our discussions here is not that we have an infinite number of Reinhold Niebuhrs but that we're beginning to come to some kind of consensus about Niebuhr's general position."

Having said this, Lovin proceeded to sketch Niebuhr's "general position." "First of all, Niebuhr's work shows an underlying commitment to public discussion about human nature and the human good. Certainly Niebuhr says a great deal about power and ideology that could be interpreted as a rejection of that kind of discussion, as moving toward a more 'realistic,' interest-group kind of politics. But when we see how Niebuhr goes about making his case for his kind of realism, then we see how much that case depends on engaging people in substantive discussion about the human good rather than the interest-group, power-based approach to politics. With all of his emphases on power, with all of his instruction on how we have to be careful about the overuse of ideals in public discussion, Niebuhr nevertheless has a clear commitment to the role of theological concepts in broader public discussion."

"Second, we see in Niebuhr's work a sociology of our common human situation that has implications for how we go about dealing with religion in public discourse. The sociology that Niebuhr gives us precludes religiously exclusive truth-claims. It also tends to exclude a religious politics. Truth, for Niebuhr, is true in relation to the whole of experience, which includes a dimension of general revelation. Truth, for Niebuhr, includes a great deal that is quite specific to the shared social situation of people in any given place in time. In the context of that sociological understanding of how we can have and not have the truth, politics is not, as Leo Strauss would have it, a search for truth. Rather, politics is an approach to practical choices that has to proceed on the basis of a holistic understanding of truth. What Niebuhr gives us in his sociology is a view of our embeddedness in history and in our communities. Niebuhr fully understands the encumbered self and would not understand the unencumbered self of original-position arguments. But Niebuhr has a suspicion of all of our claims to virtue, which extends of course to claims of virtue that might be made by Christians in the Christian community. Always we are less complete embodiments of those theological ideals than we take ourselves to be in our more pretentious moments. Our grasp of Christianity is always perspectival. If Reinhold Niebuhr could read George Lindbeck . . ."

"But maybe he can," Neuhaus suggested, provoking a chorus of laughter.

Only one person wasn't laughing—John Cuddihy. "Perhaps we laugh because we don't actually believe," he commented thoughtfully. With that, the ruckus died down, and Lovin resumed.

"What Niebuhr would want to challenge in Lindbeck would be the notion and possibility of creating a Christian community and language that would be sufficiently distinct from the surrounding culture so that we could be confident of our claims to embody that tradition and to pass it on in a way that would sharply set us apart from the surrounding culture. Niebuhr's sociology of our common human situation imposes the necessity of understanding our appropriations of Christian tradition in a larger social context.

"The practical result of that sociology is that our religious ideas can never provide us with a complete basis for politics. Their application to situations always has to be based on a fuller range of truths than the religious tradition itself bears. Niebuhr's repeated complaint against those who take religious ideals as a program of action or as a simple historical possibility is grounded in the notion that we don't have the possibility of a simple Christian politics in a given situation. A full politics will include some reference to the truths about human nature and human destiny that we understand in a Christian context, but it must necessarily develop the implications of those truths in relation to a wider framework of knowledge.

"So," Lovin concluded, "the question for Niebuhr and for anybody who works within the framework of liberal Protestantism as he does is this: What, if anything, is the distinctive contribution that faith has to make to public discourse? Niebuhr provides a kind of answer to that question that's often missing in other forms of liberal Protestantism. It assumes that there's a general, commonly held stock of rational truths into which religious language can be translated without remainder. The emphasis on temporality and finitude that is central to Niebuhr's understanding of us as human beings could serve to make us exclusively creatures of a limited time and place. But it is in the context of this emphasis that Niebuhr stresses the role of the imaginative and suprarational elements in Christianity as an essential element in sustaining a political discourse that won't simply degenerate into the conflict of interested groups. Thus, despite all of his arguments against sentimentality and naiveté, the ideal remains an essential element of Niebuhr's understanding of public discourse.

"Niebuhr was fond of saying that, with respect to American political history, our practice is wiser than our theory. That may well be a good way of summarizing my own view of Niebuhr's theoretical understanding of public discourse. There is in Niebuhr's theoretical approach to politics a good deal that reminds one of the procedural republic, and a good deal of what Lindbeck would dismiss as the experiential-expressivist approach. But the practice of public discourse, as Niebuhr understood it, implies something different. It implies a wiser theory —one that we might well take with us beyond Niebuhr's time and perhaps into our own time, as we think about the relevance of religion to public discourse."

Lovin's rather sympathetic treatment of Niebuhr's relevance was followed by Stanley Hauerwas's rather unsympathetic treatment. "What I tried to do in my paper," Hauerwas began, "is set Niebuhr's anthropology in a wider context. I'm not just starting with Niebuhr's understanding of man with anxiety as a finite creature caught with a sense of the knowledge that he is a finite creature, creating the anxiety that necessarily results in the attempt to secure significance against the finiteness, et cetera, et cetera, et cetera." That understanding of the human condition, according to Hauerwas, is taken from your basic garden-variety German idealism.

Here Hauerwas inserted a personal note: "Niebuhr taught us how to think. He gave us the categories that we've thought with for years. But I've slowly tried to train my way out of thinking in those categories. That's a very hard task, because when you let someone set the problem, oftentimes you keep getting their answer. So the challenge is how not to let them set the problem anymore. It's very hard to reset problems and reset issues. But I thought one of the ways to do that—what I tried to do in my paper—was to go at Niebuhr in terms of his global philosophy of history, in the sense that that was the fundamental way to set up what Christian ethics is about."

"Karl Lowith's article,* short though it was, raised the central issue that had never been addressed—namely, Niebuhr's attempt to situate Christianity in terms of a philosophy of history was really a way of rewriting Christian eschatology. So, according to Niebuhr, a philosophy of history becomes the way Christians now talk about eschatology. I take that to be a fundamental mistake.

" 'We are confronted with the task of reorientating the culture of our day,' " Hauerwas said, quoting Niebuhr. Then he jabbed, "Neuhaus loves that kind of phrase. And that's just what I don't like. The assumption is that fundamentally Christianity is to be culturally reorientating for the whole world. And that assumption turns Christianity into the most civil religion the world has ever encountered."

Neuhaus, in good humor, replied, "I plead innocent. I don't believe any such thing."

Hauerwas then gave Niebuhr a little credit—but just a lit-

---

*"History and Christianity," which appears in *Reinhold Niebuhr: His Religious, Social, and Political Thought*, ed. Charles Kegley and Robert Bretall (New York: Macmillan, 1956), pp. 281-90.

tle. "Niebuhr's work contains some very haunting passages on the nature of memory and why memory is so important for the moral life. If the gospel is a historically contingent matter of fact, then as a matter of fact the only way it can be present in the world is through the continuation of a people of memory. After all, the only way a historically contingent matter of fact is transmitted is through one person telling another. This reminds me of a clothing store in South Bend called Gilbert's. Gilbert's was one of those old, traditional men's stores that has very handsome clothing. In their TV ads they plugged the way people learned about Gilbert's—'one man tells another.' Now you have to get past the irony of advertising on television as the way 'one man tells another.' And a further irony is that Gilbert's left its former location and is now in a mall. But the slogan makes a point, and if you think about it, that's the way Christianity works: one person has to tell another. The Christian faith continues through the continued memory of a people. Niebuhr has very strong commitments that almost make him say that—but in the end he doesn't say it."

Completing his introductory remarks, Hauerwas took on that three-letter word, sin. "Some people would like to lift Niebuhr's account of sin out of his philosophy of history. They use Niebuhr as the most compelling prophet of the sinfulness of the human situation without buying into the inherently liberal Christological presuppositions of his philosophy. By 'some people' I mean people like Mike Novak, who wants to be a Catholic Niebuhrian. They want to use Niebuhr's account of sin to underwrite realist political analysis in a way that they think is consistent with their Catholic commitments to classical Christological patterns. What I'm saying is that you can't have it both ways. Michael doesn't want any possible tension between what it means to be Christian and what it means to be a political realist, just as Niebuhr didn't want any ultimate tension — except on the edge of history, and thus it's not in history in any determinative way. Therefore, you don't have to take the life of Jesus seriously. What Niebuhr does is de-politicize Christology: Jesus becomes salvation from the human condition and not the sanctifying possibility within history of a political alternative that is saving. In that sense, Novak represents a very pietistic point of view where Jesus' salvation is fundamentally a religious salvation that does not have fundamental, political correlatives.

Ironically, in that sense Niebuhr continues a very Protestant, individualistic account of the salvation that Jesus brings, one that operates from a satisfaction account of the atonement. I think that's questionable in terms of biblical warrant. "What you see in Niebuhr's account of sin is, in effect, a Protestant natural theology. People don't notice it as a natural theology today because it seems to challenge liberal theology's positive account of the human condition. But it's a natural theology because it doesn't see that the fundamental sin is unbelief in the resurrection of Jesus of Nazareth. Sin is not man's pretension overriding his finiteness. That fundamental theological mistake explains why Niebuhr has so little place for the church as a people who can stand apart from the wider society in a way that will offer a political service."

At this point Paul Ramsey couldn't restrain himself any longer. "It's impossible to recognize Niebuhr in what Hauerwas has written. If we're going to discuss this, it's going to take a long time."

"We've got some time, Paul," Neuhaus calmly assured him.

Niebuhr on Myth

Richard Fox commented on one of Niebuhr's categories of thought that might have some relevance for today: "Niebuhr's notion of myth came out of his early period. In particular, it came out of *Moral Man and Immoral Society*, in which he speaks of the necessity of the proletariat having myths that will generate action. Reason isn't going to be enough, he tells us, to provoke the working class to take action in its own interest. Consequently, it's important that myth be utilized in order to generate this kind of impetuous action — to generate the kinds of things that reasonableness alone will not provoke in people. One can even go back beyond *Moral Man* to Niebuhr's earliest writings and show how he distinguishes between poetry on the one hand and science on the other. Poetry is something that gives us a fuller understanding of human reality and real truth, he says, whereas science just gives us partial truth. One finds similar distinctions in *The Interpretation of Christian Ethics*, in which Niebuhr differentiates between portraiture and photography. Portraiture gives a fuller rendition of human reality, whereas photography freezes us in a moment, just like science.

"For Niebuhr, myth is an action-oriented, almost propagandistic instrument for generating and sparking movement, especially in the working class. But not only there. Niebuhr was always a propagandist, which I mean in a nonpejorative sense. He wanted to generate commitment and action in defense of certain ideals and certain realities. Here the neoconservative use of Niebuhr is right on target. For this is also the Niebuhr of the 1950s: he wanted people to believe intensely in America. And to thus believe, we need appropriate symbols and myths. We can't generate such belief simply by telling people it's reasonable to have it; we need to generate it in a much more powerful way."

Niebuhr doesn't use myths uncritically, Fox pointed out: "he's also willing to grant that myths distort reality. They're deceptive. Saint Paul spoke about 'deceivers yet true,' and I think that Niebuhr recognizes this to be applicable to myths. He knows the danger of mythmaking — the danger that the propaganda or the mythmaking will get out of hand, that we'll lose touch with what the real truth is. While we do our best to elucidate the truth through myth, we're always on the edge of losing the truth as well."

Fox threw out a metaphor to bolster his case on Niebuhr's use of myth. "Hauerwas has talked about the opening of *The Nature and Destiny of Man* as a playground of ideas. I want to suggest that it may be not so much a playground of ideas as a shooting gallery in which the Renaissance and the Greeks and other rationalists are the ducks. It's a mythmaking volume."

"It is!" Hauerwas exclaimed, enthusiastically reinforcing Fox's point. "It is! It's a remythologization. Some people always criticize Niebuhr for his lack of historical accuracy about the Renaissance and so on, but I don't think he was concerned with that. For Niebuhr the Renaissance symbolizes a whole set of eternal human possibilities. He knows there's more ambiguity than he's indicating. Nevertheless, he builds a shooting gallery. He wants to shoot down the targets, but he wants to keep them around too."

Sidney Callahan wanted the conferees to think very seriously about Niebuhr and myth. After all, she said, it's one thing to think, as Niebuhr does, that "Christianity is good for civilization and good for the world." It's quite another to believe that "Christianity is a true, supernatural reality that has broken into history in the Incarnation and the Resurrection." For Callahan, it all comes down to whether or not Niebuhr looks on Jesus and the Gospels as myth. If he does, Callahan said, "I'm ready to let him die. And I'm not going to pull his corpse around, like Hector around the walls of Troy."

Paul Ramsey was quick to respond: "I do believe that Niebuhr's notion of Christ and the Crucifixion is not a myth."

"And the Resurrection?" Neuhaus probed.

The Princeton academic respectfully declined to speak on the Resurrection, but he did address the cross. "To Niebuhr, the cross is not a myth," he said. "It stands at the center of history. If, among Niebuhr's contemporaries, you want to single out someone for whom that isn't the case, it would be Paul Tillich.

"The cross is a relevant impossibility that tangentially opens us up to indeterminate possibilities. Niebuhr constantly expressed that concept in this way: in collective action what you can achieve is mutual love, or mutuality. But he was profoundly convinced that in collective, familial, or any other kind of life, mutuality or mutual love tends to break down into self-centeredness, because individuals get into 'I-am-more-mutual-than-thou' contests—unless there is the relevant judgment and opening up to indeterminate possibilities of the love that was on the cross. That's the truth. And it judges us and opens us to notions of new mutualities. We have a message to deliver out of that cross—on the judgment of God, the grace of God, the power of God, and the wisdom of God that are over us in all of our strivings for justice in this world. That message has value and perennial truth."

Fox, who raised the issue of myth in the first place, challenged Ramsey. "For Niebuhr, the cross is a symbol," declared Fox. "Perhaps it's the central symbol in human history, but it's nevertheless ultimately a symbol. In the end he was less interested in the historicity of this event, the facticity of it, whether it really happened and was an actual breakthrough of the supernatural. These concepts didn't mean that much to Niebuhr. He was much more interested in viewing the cross symbolically."

At this point Roger Shinn challenged Fox: "In his encounter with Bultmann and Tillich, Niebuhr came to emphasize more and more the bloody, sweating man hanging on the cross —that real human being. The word 'myth,' which has many definitions, can refer to a story that isn't literally true but has meaning—like the Genesis story. Or it can refer to a story that's literally true but bears a weight of meaning far beyond the literal. I believe that if you're going to call the Christ event a myth—as Niebuhr often did—it's a myth in that second sense. It was very important to Niebuhr—above all in relation to Tillich and Bultmann—that the Christ event was an actual occurrence that's recorded in the Gospels."

Next Neuhaus recounted a conversation he had had with Niebuhr. Whether intended or not, his story tended to lend credence to the views of those who argued that Niebuhr saw the cross as myth in Shinn's first sense. Said Neuhaus, "The only really sustained conversation I had with Niebuhr, which I have reported in *Theology and the Kingdom of God,* was with Wolf Pannenberg. Wolf wanted to meet Niebuhr, so I called up Ursula and set a time. It was very much toward the end, in the last couple of years of Niebuhr's life. Niebuhr said he had read some of Pannenberg's work and was familiar with his theology of the future. His concluding comment to Wolf was that he was making a very big mistake. We've been through all of that business about the kingdom of God in this country, Niebuhr said, and it doesn't get you anywhere except bad places. If I could do it, he continued, I'd eliminate it from the Christian story—even the language of the kingdom. Maybe Niebuhr was just having a bad day. But I was very impressed by what he said—and, quite frankly, disappointed. Of course, this comment can't be taken as the definitive Niebuhrian posture on this question, but it's a statement that merits attention."

Stanley Hauerwas worried that the entire project of mythmaking is mistaken because there's a constant danger that the created myth will overpower the given story—even the Christian story—on which it is allegedly based. In other words, mythmakers might well not return to the original story. Hauerwas also expressed concern about the reasons a community or an individual has for deciding to opt for the mythmaking project in the first place. Those reasons, Hauerwas implied, are suspect.

Theological Potpourri

During this part of the Lovin-Hauerwas session, various theological matters came up and were addressed with varying degrees of thoroughness.

For some time George Weigel had been mulling over that three-letter word and Hauerwas's understanding of it. Finally he made his musings public: "Hauerwas says that an individual isn't sinful, in the way that Christians understand sinfulness, until he or she has a chance to reject Jesus. In other words, from a Christian point of view, individuals have to be trained to see themselves as sinful, because 'sin' is a word that's peculiar to Christians as it works within a very particular set of convictions."

Neuhaus inserted, "As Saint Paul said, 'I did not know sin until I heard the law.' "

Hauerwas offered an explanation: "We can be despicable and we will oftentimes use our God-given freedom to be unjust in ways that draw on our presumption that we're not God's creatures. But the way that we learn to understand our nature as sinners is through revelation. You see, 'original sin' is a very dangerous phrase. It works only within the context of Christian revelation. Therefore, contrary to what Niebuhr thought, original sin isn't a kind of myth that provides a general category through which you can tell people what they already know but haven't yet articulated. That's a mistake. 'Original sin' isn't just a universal principle—all people have sinned by their very being. Rather, it claims that whenever I'm confronted by the gospel, I always find myself in sin because of who I am—because I'm a being who isn't disposed to acknowledge myself as creature."

Stepping back to get the big picture of Niebuhr and twentieth-century Protestant thought, Paul Ramsey had this to say: "There were two major ways to be influenced by Reinhold Niebuhr and other so-called neo-orthodox figures when they were passing from the scene. My position represented one way. I felt there was more to be said about just war than Niebuhr was able to say. That's why I mined the common Christian tradition and especially Catholic wisdom. The other way — and this period may be passing, but its damage is irretrievable to the Protestant church — was situation ethics. Barth, Brunner, and Niebuhr were hesitant about coming into the new era after 1965. That's exactly Joseph Fletcher's argument; he asserted, furthermore, that we must take love as the single situationally decisive matter in Christian ethics. Ironically, what I did was simply ask my Christian brothers whether we ought not hold open the possibility that certain rules in Christian ethics are exceptionless. In other words, I was asking whether we needed to hold that all rules are open to exceptions. I was making a very modest claim, but I got nobody to support it in the days of a triumphant situationalism.

"The terrible plight of Protestantism," Ramsey sadly reported, "is that these two positions exhausted the alternatives. The continued triumph of situationalism and relativism in Protestant culture—in seminaries in particular—is disastrous beyond measure."

"But Niebuhr gave a kind of implicit endorsement of moral and sexual relativism by not going public with the kind of position that you're defending," Richard Fox charged.

"You can't argue from silence," Ramsey objected.

"I don't mean to," Fox replied. "I just mean that one could think, in the absence of proof to the contrary, that situationalism was carrying Reinhold Niebuhr forward at that point."

Then it was Roger Shinn who spoke: "Are you, Stanley Hauerwas, and Karl Lowith both modern Marcionites? Let me quickly say that I don't believe in burning heretics at the stake. But don't both of you deny any connection between the Old Testament and the Christian gospel? That is, consider the main prophetic theme—that there is a judgment as a grace of God operative in the history of the nations which is very mysterious and very incomplete short of the eschaton. There it is—the Assyrians are the rod of God's anger, but the Assyrians too will be judged. Isn't all that something you, Stanley, and Lowith deny? Also, if sin is fundamentally unbelief in the Resurrection of Jesus Christ, what were the Old Testament prophets denouncing? Probably not sin."

Trying to remove a little of the sting of his attack, Shinn added, "Stan and I have had these interchanges before. There's more geniality in them than it might appear."

"With that caution we brace ourselves," Neuhaus observed.

Shinn returned the conference to business: "The theme of this conference has to do with the right ordering of the world. Is Stan saying that that's a mistake, that Christians aren't really interested in that, that Christians have no responsibility to work for better public policies? Lowith said that Christianity is essentially indifferent to world-historical differences, and he said this in the early aftermath of World War II. At that time Niebuhr certainly refused to say that the Western side represented Christian civilization and all of that. But there is a difference—and here I'm speaking for Niebuhr and myself—between a Nazi state and a state that doesn't try to destroy the Jewish people. Can Christianity be essentially indifferent over against world-historical differences of that magnitude?"

Hauerwas took on the Marcionite indictment first. He said, "This involves Christological issues that show Niebuhr to be a paradigmatic Protestant liberal, who, as a result, is always inherently anti-Semitic. I know that sounds very odd, given Niebuhr's very early commitment to Israel and his defense of and admiration for the Jews."

"And his position against the Christian conversion of the Jews," added Shinn.

Hauerwas went to work contra Marcion: "What Niebuhr wants to do, as oftentimes Christianity has, is to make Christ a symbol, a solution to an eternal human problem such that he can explicate his Christology in a way that he finally doesn't have to make Jesus explicable within Judaism. I'm dead set against that. As I see it, you can't separate Christology from a typological interpretation of it through the Hebrew Scripture. So Niebuhr's discussion of Christology is precisely a way to avoid the significance of Jesus as the Jewish Messiah. By making Christ an eternal symbol, Niebuhr solves the eternal human predicament in such a way that he doesn't have to deal with the historical particularities of Israel, to which Jesus came.

"I don't think you can do that. I think it's decisive to know who Jesus is and that he died as Israel's Messiah. Therefore, I think that the Old Testament is, in a fundamental way, a Christian book. Niebuhr does not in fact do any typological interpretation of the Hebrew Scripture to see Jesus prefigured in it. That has a lot to do with his inability to appreciate the Trinity. Instead, what he accepts fundamentally is the way the biblical critics, who were Protestant liberals, taught him to read the Old Testament.

"So I'm not the Marcionite. On the contrary, Niebuhr is. That's one of the things that Protestant liberals haven't faced up to. Christians want to be condescending to the Jews. We want to celebrate their continued existence. But if we really took seriously Romans 9–11, we would believe that God has us in the world primarily to make the Jews jealous because they carry God's promise. But we don't believe that because we don't believe in that kind of historical particularity. As a result, Jesus as the Jews' Messiah and what that means for the historical existence of the Christian people are only given secondary display."

Shinn responded to Hauerwas. "I wish Abraham Heschel were here to make the point. But since he isn't—or since I don't now hear him—I'll ask you: Why do you find it inconsistent to say both that Jesus was the Messiah of Israel and that 'God was in Christ reconciling the world'?"

"I don't find that inconsistent," Hauerwas replied. "All I'm saying is that insofar as you construe 'God was in Christ reconciling the world' as a way of talking about what Jesus did for the universal human condition without telling the story of Israel, you will be pushed in a Christologically gnostic direction. That direction assumes that what saves is a kind of knowledge—not a particular historical person and not a particular historical people, the church. This position is hard to take because we're all liberals. It's very hard for me to say these things, even though I believe them."

Hauerwas went on to single out another issue. "Now, what do you do with the prophets' challenge of sin? Actually, that challenge doesn't come only from the prophets. You find it very early in the Pentateuch and straight through the Bible. Sin is fundamentally not doing the will of God, which is to obey his spokesmen. Of course, when Israel disobeys God, it is sinning."

Aha, said Neuhaus. "Then is sin only not believing in the risen Jesus?"

"I say that only to be as confrontational as I can," Hauerwas answered. "But then I have to spell out what the Resurrection of Jesus means in a way that the God who has created the world and has called Abraham, Isaac, and Jacob is the God of the Resurrection."

"So," Neuhaus suggested, "those who sinned in the centuries before Jesus were in fact—because of the prefigurement of Jesus—refusing to believe in the Resurrection of Jesus."

For a change, Hauerwas agreed with Neuhaus.

Shinn also wanted to know if Hauerwas thought this conference was a mistake. Hauerwas answered with characteristic vitality: "When people ask, 'Aren't you interested in the right ordering of the world?,' what a phrase they're using! The implication is that if I'm not interested in the right ordering of the world, then somehow or other I can't say that there's a fundamental difference between Nazi Germany and Switzerland. But there is! I don't need a theory about the right ordering of the world to be able to point out such a difference. I believe with Barth that we don't live in a world in which all cats are gray. But that doesn't mean that, in order to be able to make those political discriminations, I have to generate out of the gospel a theory of state legitimacy and/or a means of proving that democracies are better than the alternatives. What those kinds of questions always ask one to do is to undertake the Constantinian project. I'm not going to do that—but my refusal to do so doesn't mean that I'm saying, 'The hell with the world.' Because of the content of our faith, we Christians have obligations to serve the neighbor. And we can display that in many ways.

"I believe that our job is to try to be the kind of people who will be faithful to God and thus, it is to be hoped, will serve in God's providential care of the world. I believe that God providentially cares for the world. He will even use competing egoisms, in the Niebuhrian sense, to make the world less horrible. If my believing that means I have an indifferent attitude, so be it."

Ron Sider attempted to do some bridge-building: "Why don't you say the following, Stan? 'The core of the gospel is the good news of the kingdom. The kingdom involves a new community which is a new social order that will be completed at the eschaton. Then the whole created order will be truly transformed.' That says that God is concerned with the right ordering of the world. Furthermore, whenever we erect even modest signs of positive political change, we're moving things a little bit in the way in which they'll finally be completed. So of course Christians are concerned with the right ordering of the world. But what we mustn't do in the process—and this is what the church has regularly done—is sell out the particularity of Jesus' teaching for short-term political effectiveness. Is that what you mean when you say that you're not interested in the right ordering of the world?"

"I mean at least that," responded Hauerwas.

"So why don't you grant that we are of course interested in the right ordering of the world?" challenged Sider.

Again, Hauerwas was ready with a reply: "Because when

people say that, they always become Constantinian. They want you to play the game of responsibility. Aha, they say, you're not being responsible! But, because of Niebuhr, responsibility carries a whole set of presumptions that I don't want to accept."

At this point Ramsey spoke in favor of Niebuhr and on behalf of responsibility. "I haven't the slightest notion that Niebuhr thought that we could make history come out right. But he did think that people could take significant action in a particular time, that responsible action was possible. Niebuhr was no survivalist, nor was he a utilitarian calculator. He was a responsibilist. 'And now we come,' he would have thought, 'in the rise and fall of nations and empires, to another time. And in this particular hour a call is issued.' " And that call is a call to responsibility, Ramsey indicated.

Setting aside responsibility (at least in a way), Hauerwas added, "There's an important difference between what I mean by 'kingdom' and what Niebuhr means by it. For Niebuhr the kingdom is always an ideal that stands over against any possible realization in history. What that means is that he doesn't have any concrete manifestation of God in history. He just has the ideal standing over against historical realities. And I don't know if you need Jesus for that project."

"So," Neuhaus suggested, "with some Roman Catholics you're agreeing that the church is the historical, palpable, empirical appearance of the kingdom, the perfect society in an imperfect world."

"Of course," was Hauerwas's ready reply.

Since the conversation had moved in a distinctly ecclesiastical direction, Robert Hood of General Theological Seminary wanted to know more about Hauerwas's doctrine of the church. Hood had suspicions about Hauerwas's approach. "When Professor Hauerwas speaks of the church," he said, "it appears to be a very voluntaristic, largely atomized thing, made up of individuals. This contrasts with a more Catholic view, which says that in the church there is a givenness of tradition and an embodiment through which the church can enter into the shaping of the ordering of society, quite apart from whether all its members agree with it or not."

Hauerwas surprised his questioner and all others present with his response: "I don't believe in the individual—that's a myth of the Enlightenment. Originally the word 'individual' came from logic in the seventeenth century and had to do with certain isolated entities of a logical sort. Then it became applied politically, and I think mistakenly. It's a very misleading notion. "Nor do I think that the church is voluntaristic. That's a way that sociologists taught us to describe what it means to be called to new birth. But I do believe that the church is a called body of people who have accepted the transition, through baptism, from one world to another. As a result—and this is my way of putting it—a church isn't interesting if it doesn't tell you what to do with your pots, pans, money, and genitals. What that means is that when you're baptized into the body of Christ, you make your body available to everyone in the church. That's the reason I take the problem in 2 Corinthians to be such a severe problem. As a matter of fact, the Corinthians were involved in sexual immorality because they took that challenge so seriously.

"I take the corporateness of the church very seriously. If we could reclaim that as Christians today, we would make an extraordinary gift in service to our society. It would be a way of reminding our highly voluntaristic, individualistic world that that way of living isn't what we were created for. So don't accuse me of being a sectarian withdrawalist from a voluntaristic, individualistic world when I want the church to be the kind of body that can remind the world of how far it is away politically from what it means for people to care for one another as members of a community."

Hood, not completely satisfied, followed up: "But there are structures and forces which shape things that have very little to do with individuals."

Hauerwas agreed, then considered the case of economics. "Economics is a power that possesses us in terms of the structures in which we exist. Rather than trying to figure out how to run the American economy more justly—and God knows I don't even know how to describe the American economy—the Roman Catholic bishops might, as a start, have talked about why we, as Christians in the church, seem so incapable of sharing our incomes with one another."

At this point Neuhaus broke in, claiming that Hauerwas has a "fanatical ecclesiology" and declaring, "Stan's church is impossible. It doesn't exist."

"Of course it does," Hauerwas responded.

Neuhaus inquired, "Where empirically is this community of fidelity that you speak of?"

"Wherever God creates it," replied Hauerwas. "You can't say the church doesn't exist, Richard. After all, it's part of the creed that we say."

Neuhaus defended his position: "I'm not saying that the church doesn't exist. It does exist — but it doesn't fit your description. It happens to be your church by grace alone, despite your theological errors." That brought some uneasy chuckles.

"But," William Lazareth interjected, "the issue is where the risen Christ is today, and whether or not there are means of grace in which the risen Christ is identifiable. I can't say where the church is. But I can say where the people of God are—gathered around the risen Christ. This, Stan, you can't or won't say."

"Of course I can," Hauerwas objected. "Every Sunday when we celebrate the Eucharist we obviously are gathered around the risen Christ."

Neuhaus responded, "But the chief mark of the church for you, Stanley Hauerwas, is ethical fidelity. Indeed, the politics of Jesus *is* salvation."

"That's right," Hauerwas agreed. "And salvation includes the right preaching of the Word, the service of the sacraments, and the holiness of the community."

Neuhaus pressed his case: "And without Jesus' politics of the community, can it still be the church?"

"Certainly. God can make it the church," Hauerwas confessed with not a little faith.

With that, the day's dispute over ecclesiology ended. However, the Neuhaus-Hauerwas conversation on the church certainly hasn't ended. Their future conversations on this topic will, it is hoped, sort out what Neuhaus called "the politics of Jesus" and what Hauerwas called "the holiness of the community."

Niebuhr as Mentor, Niebuhr as Model

Opening the final part of the conference, Richard Neuhaus urged the participants to evaluate Niebuhr. "Should Reinhold Niebuhr be a major mentor in Christian social ethics in the twenty-first century? Will he be? And on both counts, your reasons, please."

Hands went flying up all over the room.

Ron Sider was the first to be identified. "I tend to believe that in very basic theological ways Niebuhr is a part of modern theological liberalism," said Sider. "That's why I find it especially funny that some evangelicals who have enormous theological differences with Niebuhr are at this point in time rushing to him. But as I look at the long history of the church, I realize that one of our worst failings is our failure to be Jesus' radical new messianic community. We have fundamentally sold out to the surrounding society. Niebuhr's lack of a doctrine of the church and the Spirit leads to a lack of integrity in the church." And a church without internal, communal integrity, Sider suggested, is ill-equipped for ministry in the public square. This rather negative general evaluation of Niebuhr for the future notwithstanding, Sider said he admired bits and pieces of Niebuhrian wisdom— for example, his thinking about power.

George Weigel testified next: "I think Reinhold Niebuhr should be one significant mentor as we move into the post-liberal era. After all, he was an exponent and a critic of the Schleiermacher project and what came out of that. But he is also a twentieth-century expression of classic Augustinian intuitions, in the Great Tradition, focused on and illuminating problems—particularly in world politics—that aren't going to disappear in the next hundred years." Among those problems, Weigel noted, are totalitarianism, maldistribution of power, and the quest for community. Then Weigel wisely observed that if Niebuhr is to endure, he can't be treated like a sacred cow. Indeed, much about Niebuhr needs to be demythologized. His "creedal lacunae" need to be met head on. His lack of a systematic framework for making moral judgments needs to be faced. In sum, declared Weigel, "this dialectical thinker must himself be put in dialectical conversation with a Murray or a Hauerwas. Out of that rubbing together and grinding will come a very interesting contribution."

William Lazareth was next in line. He voted for Niebuhr as model, not for Niebuhr as mentor. Then he explained why: "I think that Niebuhr provides us with a very helpful corrective, but in no way can he be a constitutive thinker for the twenty-first century. His analysis of power and sin, however ambiguous, is a perennial corrective to dispositions that rationalize natural law in the wrong way. But he can't be understood apart from a normative stance that he himself presupposes and that we are called to make far more articulate.

"I don't think that Niebuhr has a defensible eschatology in which symbols must be qualitatively distinguished from signs. And because there are no signs of the inbreaking kingdom for Niebuhr—only symbolical, interpretative, hermeneutical tools for evaluating experience—there's no place for the kingdom being prefigured in the people of God gathered around the risen Christ, as a model for true community as well as the realization of true personhood.

"You can't understand Kierkegaard other than as a corrective to the culture religion of Denmark. And Kierkegaard is to the culture religion of Denmark what Niebuhr is to Rauschenbusch and the American Social Gospel. But nobody reads Rauschenbusch too much anymore. In short, Niebuhr is a gloss on the classical Thomistic tradition with the kind of Augustinian realism that must be continually used to demythologize natural law in terms of the law of creation."

"That's a pretty harsh indictment, Bill," said Neuhaus—to which Lazareth didn't object.

William Miller took the position opposite Lazareth's. "I think Niebuhr should be a mentor," he confessed, "and I very much hope he will be, specifically to American society in its age of great world-dominating power."

Thank goodness, implied Miller, we don't have to worry about today's utopians coopting Niebuhr as mentor. "The utopians are among us, all right, but they don't read Niebuhr. They don't understand him— they're outside a Niebuhrian community of discourse. For example, recently I was talking to someone who works for a well-known magazine that Niebuhr founded. He asked me, 'Why do you admire this man so much?' I was stunned."

What we do have to worry about, continued Miller, is rescuing Niebuhr from the other direction. "Niebuhr needs to be rescued from the conservatives and neoconservatives who have sliced him apart, taken the realism, and jettisoned the application of that realism to its primary objects, which are the bourgeoisie, American capitalism, and the disproportion of power in modern business life. I read that emphasis all the way through Niebuhr. There's a certain sense in which he is simultaneously a supporter of and the greatest critic of the Social Gospel. According to the

Social Gospel, unthoughtful American culture had Christianity soaking into it somehow. The Social Gospel came up with the idea that people can be treated unjustly by the way in which social structures work. At the level of thinking about what a very powerful nation does both internally and externally, the Social Gospel, despite all its naiveté, wasn't so bad. But Niebuhr provided an enormous corrective of that perspective in that he saw the complexity involved when social justice is the objective. He saw how every agent of social justice is itself going to require judgment and correction as a source of injustice.

"I think Reinhold Niebuhr is a political thinker," Miller went on. "But let's hit that a little harder and say it the way Adlai Stevenson used to—'POLEitical.' That's dignity by pronunciation! There aren't a lot of political thinkers around; churches don't cast up many. Earlier in this century there were some good theologians, but Niebuhr wasn't quite that. That's why he's so vulnerable to all of these points you theologians bring up. As far as I'm concerned, Niebuhr is primarily a political thinker. I think he can be treated—I hope this won't shock everybody when I say it—outside the Christian context. Hans Morgenthau, who diminishes Niebuhr a lot and fouls him up a bit, and many other political thinkers have said that Niebuhr got it right in relation to capitalism, Marxism-communism, and other great movements of our time.

"The old Social Gospelers, with all of their faults, kept a very important set of issues in front of people. To a certain extent those issues have strayed off into various utopian projects. But partly—and this is dominant today—the conservatives and neoconservatives have taken over those issues. Here in the final days of the Reagan era—and pardon the partisanship—there is a kind of embodiment of the things Niebuhr started out attacking, the bourgeois capitalist ethos. Look at careerism and Wall Street and the assumption that somehow supply and demand will naturally solve problems. Niebuhr was a good critic of that. He always kept ready the criticism of the criticism. He was like George Orwell, another good political thinker. He was a virtuous man whose mind was mainly occupied with the great movements of politics. And he did this kind of thinking very well. That his perspective was significantly shaped by his being a Christian preacher—sure, that's very important. That's part of the reason he got it right."

Paul Ramsey objected to what he perceived to be Miller's Niebuhr: "If we take Niebuhr as a purely 'POLEitical' theorist, my unhappy thought is that without transcendent reference his view of politics would be the war of all against all. If you seek only justice—without love—you've got war, because there is no universal view of justice. Transcendence opens our views of justice up to indefinite possibilities of greater mutuality." And that, contended Ramsey, is what Niebuhr believed, preached, and wrote.

Miller responded to Ramsey's rebuttal: "Arthur Schlesinger and others have said that you could pretty well leave Niebuhr's theology behind and take his politics and run with it. I'm not saying that. Niebuhr wouldn't be at all what he was if he hadn't been a Christian thinker with transcendent reference who believed in the love-justice dialectic. In fact, the love-justice link is 'POLEitically' significant."

Theodore Weber was still unsatisfied with Miller's sketch of Niebuhr. "I don't think Niebuhr can be thought of as becoming a purely secular thinker and still remain Reinhold Niebuhr. Niebuhr's power does not lie primarily in his social analyses, although those were, for the most part, astute. His power lies in the fact that he was able to look into the depths of human nature, human experience, and the structure of society with his theology — whether mythological or not. He was able to say, 'There is more mystery in human existence, there are more depths to human existence, there are more contradictions in human existence, there are more possibilities that come from outside human existence and are mediated through it than you are able to see with secular political analyses alone.' If we take that away from Niebuhr, he is no longer Reinhold Niebuhr."

Weber then talked about how Niebuhr might be and should be a mentor for today and tomorrow. "Something like *Moral Man and Immoral Society* is a necessity for any political movement, and especially for any movement that claims to have Christian inspiration. Two of my colleagues who occasionally visit Emory are Jürgen Moltmann, representing German political theology, and José Míguez Bonino, representing Latin American liberation theology. I press both of them on the matter of when they or someone in their respective movements is going to get around to doing the job on their movements that Reinhold Niebuhr did on American socialism and American religious socialism in the

1930s. They're not buying it, perhaps because they figure they'll come out the same way he did—with some real pessimism about what the possibilities are. But that's a necessary task. And it's a theological task as well as a politically necessary task, so I'll continue to press my two colleagues on this point."

Weber went on to offer some oral tradition about Moltmann: "Somebody once mentioned that the first theological book that Moltmann read was *The Nature and Destiny of Man* and that it made a tremendous impression on him. So I once asked Moltmann about this. He explained that he had been a prisoner of war in England. After Moltmann had worked for a time in the coal mines, the British set up a seminary for Germans who wanted to be pastors. For a year or so Moltmann attended that school. The first assigned work of 'dogmatic theology,' as he put it, was Reinhold Niebuhr's *Nature and Destiny of Man*. But that was forty years ago, he pointed out, and he had forgotten the book." Indeed he has, Weber noted.

Weber went on to list Niebuhrian contributions that remain useful: in particular his critique of self-deception, messianism, and righteousness; his critique of the attempt to control history (such attempts, said Niebuhr, should be greeted with the biblical text "He that sitteth in the heavens shall laugh"); and his emphases on love and justice, discriminating moral-political judgments, and the transforming power of the cross. But Weber wanted to make clear that he wasn't pushing for an uncritical, uninterpreted employment of Niebuhr for today. He put today's Niebuhrian project on sturdy theological footing: "The beginning point today is the church with its self-understanding and its awareness of its witness and mission. Then, in the light of that understanding, the church can raise the question about what is to be done about our relationship to American society. The love that motivates and requires us to make discriminating judgments grows out of a Christological context by which we know that the power of God is sure and has been revealed in Jesus Christ. It transforms our relationship with the neighbor, even though we're not yet aware of it. This is the way to do a reconstruction of Niebuhr for today. Then bring in some of the Niebuhrian elements of anthropology, wisdom, and realism. This is better than trying to separate Niebuhr from theology and trying to find out what we can do in a secular fashion with this brilliant political critic."

Richard Hutcheson's position was unambiguous. "Reinhold Niebuhr must be a major mentor as we move ahead," he declared. "When Christians try to address the problems of a right world order and the legitimating of democracy in the face of perceived internal and external attacks, they face — in a pluralistic society like ours — enormous contradictions and obstacles. We have in Niebuhr a Christian thinker of our age who addressed these issues very powerfully and very effectively. I'm not bothered by the fact that we take pieces of Niebuhr's work while rejecting some of the underlying assumptions, because those pieces are so important to the way we address public policy. Those pieces help to provide an understanding of power, justice, the significance of sin, the relevance of biblical images in public life, and the necessity of a prophetic critique along with active involvement. These are central issues. Accordingly, I believe Niebuhr should be seen as more than a model. I believe he should be seen as a mentor."

Richard Fox also saw Niebuhr as a mentor. "Niebuhr is a modernist," he explained. "*Leaves from the Notebook of a Tamed Cynic* is a great, classic text. It was written by a man who realized when he was very young that he was already a post-Christian. He doubted himself as a Christian, and he doubted the church as a saving institution. From a very young age he lived very much on a boundary, much as Tillich always claimed that he was on a boundary. He doubted himself very profoundly: he always described himself as an unbelieving believer. His father, he told us, was a doubting Thomas. The fact that Niebuhr considered himself to be on this boundary line between belief and unbelief, between the church and the secular world, is precisely why he is relevant today. He is uniquely able to speak to those who consider themselves purely secular. He is able to raise doubts in their minds. Likewise, he is able to raise doubts in the church about the relevance of religion."

Neuhaus, evidently in a mood to do some free association, asked, "Does anybody have any evidence that Niebuhr prayed in the ordinary sense—aside from going to church?"

"That's really a hard one," Fox replied. "I tried to figure that one out, and I couldn't do it to my satisfaction. I don't believe it's possible to claim that he prayed the way he said his father prayed—by reading the Bible daily in Greek. I don't think one could say that Niebuhr didn't pray, but I doubt that he very often got down on his knees and prayed, because he was largely a secular man. I doubt that he significantly rested from his daily actions in order to pray. His action was his prayer."

"But he wrote a lot of prayers," Roger Shinn countered, "and he began and ended his sermons with prayer."

"And one ought to read his prayers and ask whether it's credible to believe that he didn't pray," challenged Paul Ramsey.

"No, it isn't," said Stanley Hauerwas. "I've been driving back and forth between the University of Virginia and Duke, and I've been listening to the cassette tapes of Niebuhr that are available from Union Theological Seminary in Richmond. I've listened to all of his recorded sermons as well as his courses— and you can't tell me he didn't pray. I've heard him pray after his sermons, so I know that man prayed. I don't have any doubt. He never prayed to the congregation; he prayed to God."

"And he didn't just repeat his sermon," Ramsey chuckled, poking fun at a common pastoral practice.

At this point the conferees began to do some free association about Niebuhr's role as preacher. William Miller recalled being in Santa Barbara in the 1960s with Niebuhr. "At the time Niebuhr was rather gloomy and self-critical about his whole project. It was around that time, he said, that he had tried to sell the world on original sin, and the world hadn't bought it. But he was also saying, 'I'm a preacher.' I didn't realize until that moment that that was a very strong identity for Niebuhr. In listening to his sermons, you realize how much he was a preacher all of his life."

Hauerwas added to Miller's personal account by referring once again to the Niebuhr tapes. "On one of the tapes of a class he's teaching, Niebuhr says that he's really not much of a professor, but that he has always fundamentally been a preacher—as distinguished from a theologian. And he says that that's really what he's good at."

Shinn admitted that Neuhaus's original questions—Will and should Reinhold Niebuhr be a major mentor in Christian social ethics into the twenty-first century?—was quite intimidating. After all, Shinn pointed out, we don't know what the twenty-first century will bring. Perhaps a nuclear holocaust, or perhaps an ecological disaster, he ventured, but we don't know. But eventually Shinn shed all evidence of intimidation and launched into a systematic presentation of "four themes out of Niebuhr's ethic that will be important, no matter what."

Shinn started with "the love-justice dialectic. God has created us to love one another. A love that does not somehow get structured in law and justice is a sentimental love. Those structures do involve some coercion—not necessarily violence —and that fits strangely with love. Yet justice is never complete unless it is a loving justice. Love requires justice, and justice requires love. Tension is clearly there." Although the love-justice dialectic is not original with Niebuhr, he did make it particularly relevant to modern politics, said Shinn.

The second important theme that Shinn brought up was Niebuhr's relation of sin and grace. "I find his doctrine of sin utterly convincing in my own life and in my observation of the world," Shinn asserted. "About the time you think you've made some progress overcoming sin, you get caught up in it. Then comes the response of grace as forgiveness and power. Niebuhr is very clear on forgiveness, but we all wish he had said more about grace as power. I think the reason he didn't was honesty. So many claims for grace as power turn out to be phony. That's not to deny the power that's there, but we must be wary of claiming it. Sidney Hook was asked why, as a secularist, he so admired Niebuhr. Hook's answer was Niebuhr's resolute honesty. Niebuhr didn't claim things that were just phony.

"The third important Niebuhrian theme is that belief in the kingdom of God requires us to work for goals less than the kingdom. Get the next bill through Congress, for example, or get an administration in Washington you like better. Belief in the kingdom requires us to work for goals judged by the kingdom. I don't know of any other belief that promotes this kind of staying power. While there are certain illusions that allow people to get going and accomplish something, the thing about these historical-political fights is that we win some and we lose some, and the ones we win turn out to be not such glorious victories as we thought. That's why faith in something more than our political ideals may enable us to continue to do something."

"And the fourth significant Niebuhrian theme is the effort to relate the Christian faith to a pluralistic world. Here we can't just do it Niebuhr's way, because the world is getting increasingly pluralistic. Look at the U.N., the international arena, and American life. In the same week Niebuhr would be writing an explicitly theological piece for *Christianity and Crisis* and also a piece for *The Nation* or *The New Republic* using no theological lan-

guage at all. You could never say that Niebuhr's theological discourse translated without remainder into the secular, but much
of his work was translatable into that language."

Roman Catholic Christopher Wolfe allowed that his "contribution might seem like a parochial one, but that it might be
useful to have reports from a parochial enclave."

"But we're all in parochial enclaves, especially those of us
who think we're living universally," Neuhaus remarked.

That taken care of, Wolfe continued, "I came here largely
ignorant of Niebuhr, and I'll leave uncertain about Niebuhr on
the basis of many of the differences among you who know
Niebuhr better than I do. Am I going to go home and read
Niebuhr? First I want to distinguish between reading books to
understand history and reading books to understand reality—
not that those two things are totally different. But the practical
reality is that you can read only a limited number of books. That
means that you have to confine yourself to the best, although
you recognize that you can find something significant even in
books that aren't the very best. Accordingly, I won't go home
and read Niebuhr, although I understand why other people
would." Wolfe went on to elaborate: "Christians have to expect
from somebody who claims to provide a Christian social ethic
that he or she will be rooted in Christian orthodoxy. Everything
I've heard here today suggests that Niebuhr isn't—and that's
why I'm going to look elsewhere for guidance in Christian social ethics and political problems."

"So we can't rack you up as a sale!" Neuhaus quipped.

"No!" Wolfe answered.

John Cuddihy then implied that Niebuhr shouldn't be
taken either as a mentor or as a model. To convey his reasons for
this judgment, Cuddihy told his version of Niebuhr's life story:
"Reinhold Niebuhr was a young man from the provinces who
headed for New York, stopping off in Detroit on the way. He
wrote an article, which he followed to New York. He made a hit
and became a success. Why? Well, because he fit in. The
American clergy have always been afraid of irrelevance and
marginalization; they've been afraid of being pushed out.
They've always had to remake—in America anyway—their
role. Niebuhr had to do that. He was a preacher. Right! He was
very eloquent with words and gestures. He was a spellbinder,
almost a kind of Elmer Gantry. Preaching was what he loved.

He used a few prooftexts on sin as a kind of disedifying discourse to hold people who wouldn't be held by positive thinking. In a way he was part of a new knowledge class. What he
knew was this message and these texts. He broke in, and he was
ambitious. He was somewhat ashamed of the gospel, but he was
also ashamed of opponents of the gospel. He wasn't ashamed
to berate the rich in Detroit, but he was ashamed to berate the
Jewish community in New York. So he came as an encumbered
self. The gospel encumbered him with the message of salvation
to the Jews, to all people. So he disencumbered the gospel of its
universalism, as the message to the Jews; this stood in the way
of his success. It had to go. *That* is the story I tell about Niebuhr
in Chapter Three of my book, *No Offense.*"

Just in case someone had been napping—although nobody had been—Neuhaus summarized and sharpened Cuddihy's argument: "Jack Cuddihy contends that the virtue of
courage was remarkably absent in Reinhold Niebuhr, that basically he can be explained in terms of ambition and 'making it.'
Richard Fox tends to lend some support to that idea in his book.
According to them, Niebuhr can be seen as a man intent upon
making it, someone who very carefully never offended the con-
stituencies that mattered and that defined his status and influence. When it came to the crunch, he pulled his punches. Are
these two right—did this man lack the virtue of courage?"

Stanley Hauerwas, probably speaking representatively for
other conferees, replied, "I wouldn't presume to judge Niebuhr
on that. He did remarkable things. All I can do is see his life continued and reflected in the mentors that I have as a theologian.
They've tried to think hard about what it means to be a Christian in this society. And, by God, they certainly have a lot of
courage. If Niebuhr continues in them, then I think he had a lot
of courage."

Concluding Arguments

In his final comments, Robin Lovin engaged Hauerwas's
primary concern — the church. "A Niebuhrian notion of the
church," he began, "might well be a community of moral discourse in the most ordinary sense. If one were to try to do
Niebuhr's work in the church these days, one would express the
way the church serves as a particular community of moral dis-

course. Why? Simply because it is important that that be done. I'm enough of an orthodox Methodist to think that it's appropriate for the church to provide people with what they need in particular times in history. There were times when they needed hospitals. What they may need now is a place to engage in moral discourse. Furthermore, it's very important that the church be a place that sustains those memories of its particular stories that make sense of human experience in the course of Christian history."

Then Lovin attempted what might be called ecclesiastical realism. "But when one moves beyond that to talk about the church as a community that prefigures the kingdom, I want to see that as a symbolic possibility. But, like Niebuhr, I want to hold up against that the sociological reality within which that prefiguration of the kingdom always exists. I think about my own church setting—never mind the church at large. At church I stand in the circle with a group of people that includes a couple of welfare mothers, a commodities broker, two or three Filipino nurses, and a Filipino schizophrenic who carries a three-foot-high doll. I look around that kind of circle and I say to myself, 'Whatever it is that I share with these people, surely it's not a common story—or at least that's not all that's involved here.' We are all claimed by and drawn to that particular place by the way in which Christianity impinges upon our personal idolatries—in my case, the idolatries that I carry around with me at the University of Chicago. Christianity makes more sense for me because and as it includes all of those people, including the guy with the doll. At the same time it also includes David Tracy and Jim Gustafson."

"They may pose a bigger problem than the guy with the doll," Neuhaus noted, with humorous intent.

"What I'm trying to do," Lovin continued, "is avoid romanticizing the possibilities of this kind of community. That the kingdom is prefigured in that kind of community is an ideal possibility. As soon as we start talking about that community as a prefiguration of the kingdom, then some other kind of critical message needs to be brought to bear on that." Here Lovin was arguing against the Richard Rorty type of liberalism that urges people to shed their encumbrances, including religious encumbrances, and simply concern themselves with pragmatic adjustments of interests. At the same time Lovin was warning the conference against a gnostic-romantic ecclesiology in which the church's stories become bars and walls that imprison. "And I don't want to charge Professor Hauerwas with being a gnostic-romantic," Lovin promised.

"If you do," Neuhaus predicted, "he'll turn it against you" —just like he had turned Roger Shinn's charge of anti-Semitism against Shinn.

In the end Lovin expressed hope for a community—that is, a church—anchored soundly in human experience, even modern experience. That community must also be possessed by myths so powerful that it can transcend the thus-and-so-ness of the day and reach for imaginative possibilities that are hidden behind and between acknowledged human and historical limitations. Ideally, this community would build a reservoir of confidence for action in the world, and this action would be more than a mere critique of ideology.

Stanley Hauerwas used his time for concluding comments differently. He spoke about the tradition that he serves. "For six or seven years I've been teaching a course in which I start with Rauschenbusch and then go on to Reinhold Niebuhr, H. Richard Niebuhr, Catholic developments, Paul Ramsey, Jim Gustafson, and John Howard Yoder. I do that because I'm committed to not letting that tradition be forgotten. It is a tradition. You can't understand Ramsey unless you understand Niebuhr. You can't understand Gustafson unless you understand his background. And, interestingly enough, you can't understand John Howard Yoder unless you understand him as a post-Niebuhrian pacifist.

"In other words, from the 1890s to the present we have had an extraordinary group of people develop who started a conversation that is crucial for us all. We should continue to take part in it as Christians trying to think over the issues we confront today. But I can see that the wider society now, on the whole, doesn't want that tradition. It doesn't see that tradition as integral to public discourse today. Now I don't know how to respond except to keep that tradition in the memory of the people I train for the ministry for the church of Jesus Christ. Whether that will serve a political purpose, I don't know. But I think it's crucial to the internal nature of the church."

To be sure, as Hauerwas explained, the service of this tradition is always critical service. "This tradition has led me to be increasingly critical of the love-justice dialectic as the way to think about Christian social ethics. The love-justice dialectic tends to make social ethics too abstract from concrete people and from the institutions that need to stand over against the wider society. But I can't think that way without Niebuhr. I've got to have him; he's part of the conversation that constitutes a tradition that's crucial to me."

Hauerwas concluded with a concrete point: "One of the nicest things that we've heard here is Robin Lovin's description of his fellow church members. I don't think that that group of people is possible anywhere else outside the Christian community. I think it's wonderful that Robin stands there worshiping with a schizophrenic holding a doll. I don't see American society desiring that. That's exactly the kind of critical edge that we need."

Participants

James V. Bachman
University Lutheran Chapel
Tallahassee, FL

Charles C. Brown
Marguerite Eyer Wilbur Fellow
Columbia, MO

Sidney Callahan
Department of Psychology
Mercy College

John W. Cooper
Ethics and Public Policy Center

John Cuddihy
Department of Sociology
Hunter College

Richard Wightman Fox
Department of History
Reed College

Stanley Hauerwas
The Divinity School
Duke University

John P. Hittinger
Department of Philosophy and
    Religious Studies
College of St. Francis
Joliet, IL

Robert E. Hood
General Theological Seminary

Richard G. Hutcheson, Jr.
Senior Fellow, The Rockford
    Institute Center on Religion
    & Society

Jerome B. King
Department of Political Science
University of Massachusetts at
    Amherst

William H. Lazareth
Evangelical Lutheran Church
    in America
New York, NY

Robin W. Lovin
The Divinity School
University of Chicago

Ralph McInerny
The Medieval Institute
University of Notre Dame

William Lee Miller
Department of Rhetoric and
    Communication Studies
University of Virginia

Kenneth A. Myers
Evangelical Editor
Powhatan, VA

Richard John Neuhaus
The Rockford Institute Center
    on Religion & Society

David Novak
Baruch College
City University of New York

Paul Ramsey
Center of Theological Inquiry
Princeton, NJ

Michael J. Sandel
Department of Government
Harvard University

Roger L. Shinn
Union Theological Seminary
New York, NY

Ronald J. Sider
Eastern Baptist Theological
  Seminary

Paul T. Stallsworth
The Rockford Institute Center
  on Religion & Society

Glen E. Thurow
Politics Department
University of Dallas

Theodore R. Weber
Candler School of Theology
Emory University

George Weigel, Jr.
The James Madison Foundation
Washington, D.C.

Christopher Wolfe
Department of Political Science
Marquette University